"If you were doubting the beloved legume's superpowers, let Kathy Hester's brand new book show you that there's just nothing they can't do for you: breakfast, lunch, dinner, and even dessert. All irresistibly magical, all the time."

—Celine Steen, co-author of *Vegan Sandwiches Save the Day!*

"*The Great Vegan Bean Book* is a must-have book for any plant-powered kitchen. If you are looking to add more fiber- and protein-packed meals to your plate—simply and deliciously—this book is for you!"

—Lauri Boone, R.D., author of *Powerful Plant-Based Superfoods*

"Beans—in all their humble, uncontroversial glory—finally get the respect they're due in Kathy Hester's completely nourishing and utterly gorgeous recipes."

—Nava Atlas, author of *Vegan Holiday Kitchen*

"If you're in a bean-cooking rut, then you need this book. Kathy's bean-tastic recipes range from exquisite soups and chilies to inventive creations that extend the boundaries of bean-based cooking (Lemon Coconut Chickpea Muffins, anyone?)."

—Dynise Balcavage, author of *Pies and Tarts with Heart*

"Whether you're a card-carrying bean-lover or simply want to add more healthy and inexpensive meatless meals to your repertoire, *The Great Vegan Bean Book* is for you. With a wide variety of tempting recipes from simple to sophisticated, Kathy Hester proves that beans can be anything but boring—and even downright dazzling."

—Robin Robertson, author of *Quick-Fix Vegan*

This book is dedicated to you, my reader.
You are the one I thought of most while I was writing it.
I sincerely hope that you find some recipes and tips that
make your meals a little easier and life more delicious.

© 2013 Fair Winds Press
Text © 2013 Kathy Hester
Photography © 2013 Renée Comet

First published in the USA in 2013 by
Fair Winds Press, a member of
Quayside Publishing Group
100 Cummings Center
Suite 406-L
Beverly, MA 01915-6101
www.fairwindspress.com

17 16 15 14 13   2 3 4 5

ISBN: 978-1-59233-549-7

Digital edition published in 2013
eISBN: 978-1-61058-747-1

Library of Congress Cataloging-in-Publication
Data

Hester, Kathy.
  The great vegan bean book : more than 100
delicious plant-based dishes packed with the
kindest protein in town! most recipes are soy-
and gluten-free! / Kathy Hester.
     pages cm
  ISBN 978-1-59233-549-7
  1. Cooking (Beans) 2. Vegan cooking.
  3. Cookbooks lcgft I. Title.
   TX803.B4H49 2013
   641.6'565--dc23
                                           2012043102

Cover and book design by Debbie Berne Design
Photography by Renée Comet Photography

Printed and bound in China

THE GREAT VEGAN
BEAN
BOOK

More than 100 Delicious Plant-Based Dishes Packed
with the Kindest Protein in Town!

KATHY HESTER

Photography by Renée Comet

FAIR WINDS
P R E S S
BEVERLY, MASSACHUSETTS

CONTENTS

BEAUTIFUL BEANS

Basics, How-Tos, and Recipes to Keep Your Food Budget in Check

Almost every culture or country cooks with beans and is famous for one bean recipe or another. Any meal of your favorite cuisine can get a bean upgrade—consider Indian cooking, which features an endless amount of dishes made with beans!

Beans are full of protein and fiber while being low in fat. They are a great source of iron, copper, phosphorus, manganese, and magnesium. But they're also chock-full of thiamin, folic acid, riboflavin, and vitamin B_6. There's just so much to love about beans!

Beans can help ease the strain on a food budget. Found in any grocery store, they are typically inexpensive. You can find fancy ones in an Indian or Hispanic specialty store that are dirt-cheap as well. Although many of the heirloom beans will cost more, they are worth it for their varied tastes and textures. In many of the recipes I have a cheaper bean listed first with a fancy bean substitute you can try as well. This way you can have some great beans for dinner no matter what your food budget is.

The exceptions are the baked goods and desserts. There's no need to spend extra money on heirloom beans when you aren't going to taste them. In fact, I use blander beans so they won't overwhelm the flavor. They excel at creating a moist baked good with little or no oil at all!

In the majority of the recipes in this book, you can choose whether you want to cook your beans from scratch or use canned beans. It's more economical to use dried beans, but sometimes convenience wins out. I always have a drawer full of various common and heirloom beans, as well as cans of beans stashed in the pantry.

Dried beans are much cheaper than canned and don't contain any additives, so they are my first choice. If you are going to use canned beans, buy organic if possible. Some nonorganic canned beans have sweeteners, preservatives, coloring, and firming agents and are high in sodium. But you avoid most of that in the organic canned beans, though they still tend to contain a high amount of salt.

HOW TO COOK BEANS

All of the recipes in this book start with cooked beans unless otherwise noted, either homemade, using one of the methods that follow, or canned beans, which are ready as soon as you open the can. However, I do recommend that you rinse and drain canned beans before you use them. This washes off the tinny taste and extra salt and basically makes a healthier and tastier product for you to use as the base of your dish.

One option when making these recipes is to cook your dried beans in a slow cooker the night before and then add the rest of your ingredients in the morning. Or you can add your canned or precooked frozen beans in the morning. It's completely up to you. Whenever I offer a slow cooker option, use one that has a 4-quart (3.8-L) capacity, unless otherwise noted.

Some people have an easy time digesting beans and other high-fiber foods, but others end up having a harder time. Most people digest beans better by adding them gradually to their diet. But you can also try things like cooking beans with traditional herbs that are said to help or use some of the soaking methods. The most important thing is that you find what works best for your body. I will tell you that I think different digestive systems respond better after beans have been soaked or cooked using a particular method. So go ahead and stick with your method if you have a sensitive system and have already found that it works for you.

It is very important to cook beans all the way. Beans that are half-done or not soft enough will give everyone a stomachache, so err on the side of caution. (And, of course, there is an exception to every rule. Indians use a raw, skinned, split black lentil called urad dal as a seasoning. These are only stir-fried, making them crunchy, similar to nuts.)

The Very First Thing to Do: Inspect and Rinse

You may think that grocery store beans are triple-cleaned beans and forget to look through your beans and rinse them. This is not a good idea—ever. With many beans there are tiny rocks and other small debris that could cause a visit to the dentist. If that happens, it will take the thrifty right out of your beans!

Measure your beans and then pour them out on one side of a clean counter or cutting board. Move them a few at a time to the other side while looking for small rocks, odd-looking beans, and anything thing else that doesn't belong in your cooking pot. Then give them a quick rinse in a colander to remove any dust or dirt.

To Soak or Not to Soak?

Mexicans tend not to soak beans before cooking, while Indians almost always do. Some people soak to make the beans more digestible, and others soak merely to cut down on the cooking time.

It is thought that oligosaccharides are responsible for the gas issues associated with eating beans. Oligosaccharides are indigestible, short molecular chains of sugars that are stored in the outer coatings of legumes, nuts, and seeds. Soaking beans overnight and getting rid of the cooking water as well as the soaking water is thought to get rid of these unwanted side effects.

Note that every time you discard the soaking or cooking water out you lose some B vitamins. However, you're still getting the other nutrients in the beans that you wouldn't receive if you didn't eat them at all.

If you decide to soak your beans, put them in a bowl and cover with water until there is about 3 inches (7.5 cm) of water above the beans. Soak overnight and your beans will be ready to cook in less than half the time the next day.

You can also do what's known as a quick soak. Add beans to the saucepan and cover with water until there is about 3 inches (7.5 cm) of water above the beans. Bring to a boil, cover, turn the heat off, and move to the side to sit for 30 minutes to 1 hour. Now the beans will cook faster once you put the pot back on the heat.

Traditional Herbs That Can Help Make Beans More Digestible

Each country seems to have its own solution for the "wind" problem, such as adding different herbs to the cooking process. As with my soaking recommendation, I think you should try a few different ways and see which one works best for you. You can add these herbs during the initial cooking of the dried beans to make them most effective. But whether or not they remove the gas, the ingredients below will make your beans tastier! Here are a few ideas, any of which would work for a standard-size pot of beans (cooking 1 to 2 cups [225 to 455 g] from dry):

- 1 strip kombu—This is a dried seaweed or sea vegetable that is commonly used in Asia as well as the natural foods community.

- 2 bay leaves.

- 1 teaspoon epazote—This is an herb used frequently in Mexican cuisine. It can be found online at spice stores or in Hispanic groceries.

- 1 teaspoon ground cumin.

- a few sprigs of summer savory.

- a pinch of hing—Also known as asafetida, this is a frequent ingredient in Indian cuisine and can be found at Indian markets and online spice stores.

Cooking Methods

Split peas and lentils cook much faster than larger beans such as pinto, black, and white. They are often cooked in a recipe dry, while the larger beans are cooked before being added to the slow cooker.

STOVE-TOP METHOD: Put the beans in a saucepan and cover with water until the water is about 2 inches (5 cm) above the beans. Bring to a boil, then lower the heat to a simmer, and cook for 1 to 2 hours until the beans become tender. If the water is getting low, feel free to add more during the cooking process.

Cooking times can be considerably longer for older beans. Even if you just bought the beans at the store, they could still be old. If you prefer a more concrete measurement, you can use 3 cups (700 ml) of water to 1 cup (225 g) of beans.

OVEN METHOD: This method cooks as fast as on the stove top and doesn't need as much babysitting, so it's a little like slow cooking them. It's perfect for a cold winter day because it's a great excuse to keep the oven on.

Preheat the oven to 350°F (180°C, or gas mark 4). Add 2 cups (455 g) dried beans and 6 cups (1.4 L) water to a Dutch oven. Bring to a boil on the stove top. After the water boils, cover and place in the oven. Cook the beans for 1 to 3 hours depending on size and age. Older beans take longer to cook in all cooking methods. Check every 45 minutes to see whether more water is needed and if the beans are tender.

SLOW COOKER METHOD: You can cook any beans in the slow cooker, but be aware that kidney beans can have a toxin called *phytohaemagglutinin* and need to be brought up to a boiling temperature to destroy the toxin. Boil them for 10 minutes before cooking in the slow cooker. This step is not necessary for other types of beans.

Add the beans to the slow cooker and cover with water until the water is about 3 inches (7.5 cm) above the beans. Cook on low overnight, or for 6 to 9 hours. You have a large margin of error in the slow cooker and that's the reason it's my favorite method.

JILL NUSSINOW'S METHOD OF PRESSURE COOKING BEANS: My friend Jill Nussinow, queen of the pressure cooker, has allowed me to share her expertise with you. To get more information and recipes for your pressure cooker, go to her websites, www.theveggiequeen.com and www.pressurecookingonline.com.

You can pressure-cook dried or soaked beans, but note that unsoaked beans will take four times as long as those that have been soaked. Also, unsoaked beans require more liquid for cooking and should be completely covered with water. Although soaked black beans only take about 6 minutes when pressure-cooked, unsoaked ones take 25 minutes once the cooker reaches its full pressure. Other presoaked beans also cook quickly in a pressure cooker: pinto beans take just 4 minutes and chickpeas take 12 minutes.

Did You Know?

You can cook extra beans and freeze in bags to use later. I freeze mine in 1½-cup (340-g) portions so that it's easy to switch out a bag for a can of beans.

To cook the beans, use ¾ cup (175 ml) of water for each 1 cup (225 g) of dried beans that are presoaked (measure beans before soaking). Bring to high pressure over high heat, and then reduce the heat to maintain high pressure. Once your timer beeps, remove the pot from the heat and let the pressure come down naturally. Carefully remove the lid, tilting it away from you.

Jill only uses what's called a "modern" or "spring-valve" pressure cooker. This is not your grandma's pressure cooker with the jiggler on top that hisses and can "blow up." The new pressure cookers are quiet and reliable. They have a little button that pops up to let you know that it's time to set the timer and lower the heat to keep the pot at pressure. When your timer beeps, move the pot to a cool burner and wait for the pressure to come down naturally.

Open the lid carefully and taste the beans to see whether they are cooked through. If they are, use them. If not, replace the lid and bring the pot to high pressure over high heat again for another minute or two. It's best to let the pressure drop naturally, the beans can split open otherwise (which doesn't matter if you are making hummus or another bean dip).

BEAN-BY-BEAN COOKING TIMES

Beans come in a wide variety of shapes and sizes, and cooking times vary from type to type. I've divided this section by cooking times. Keep in mind that older beans will always take longer to cook, so these times are just to give you a general idea.

Quick-Cooking Beans

FRESH BEANS: *Cook for 15 to 30 minutes on the stove top without soaking.*
Green beans can be had fresh all year, but at certain times of the year you can find fresh black-eyed peas, purple hull beans, October beans, and other crowder peas, too. Crowder peas, or field peas, are popular in the South. The

term *crowder peas* comes from the fact that the peas seem crowded in the shell. These beans taste similar to black-eyed peas, but are not the same. You may find them at farmers' markets in the summer, fresh in their shells, or if you're lucky, already shelled.

Fresh beans cook faster, making them perfect for bean and rice dishes that you make in one pan. The Jamaican Purple Hull Peas and Rice recipe on page 166 is a perfect dish to make when these beans are in season. If you're lucky you may see some of these frozen during your winter farmers' market.

DRIED LENTILS: *Cook for 20 to 35 minutes on the stove top, depending on type, without soaking.*

Lentils are a type of bean and come in many colors and sizes. You can find almost any kind of lentils cheaper at an Indian grocery than at a regular supermarket. If you don't have one in your area, you can also find an Internet source that will deliver right to your house.

If you've never been to an Indian grocery, you may not know just how varied lentils can be. Almost every kind of lentil has four variations at the Indian grocery: whole with skin on, whole without skin, split with skin on, and split without skin.

Most dals that you get in Indian restaurants have a mix of lentils making up their base. My friend Kalpana uses as many as seven different lentils in her yellow dal! Here are some of the ones used in this book:

* **Red lentils** are also known as *masoor dal*, which are split and skinned masoor beans. When cooked down, as in soups and stews, they turn golden and disintegrate. That makes them perfect for the bean haters in your house!
* **Split green peas** are perfect for split pea soup.
* **Brown lentils** are the most common lentils used in soups, stews, and my stove-top biryani. (Biryani is an Indian rice and bean dish that varies widely in its ingredients and usually contains nuts and/or dried fruit. It may also contain saffron.)
* **French green lentils (puy lentils)** are a more delicate lentil that holds its shape well.
* **Beluga lentils** are small black lentils that are very decorative on salads and appetizers.

* **Golden petite lentils**, also known as moong dal, are actually split and skinned mung beans, but are sold in health food stores as golden petite lentils for a premium price.
* **Urad dal** are split black lentils (larger than the beluga lentils) without skins, which actually makes them white. You can find them in Indian grocery stores.

In-Between Cooking Beans

Cook for 30 minutes to 1 hour on the stove top, depending on type, without soaking. These beans take a little longer than a typical lentil to cook, but less time than kidney or pinto beans.

* **Black-eyed peas**, are a traditional Southern staple, and a must for a New Year's Day meal. Yellow-eyed peas make a great substitute to fancy up your dish.
* **Adzuki beans** are often used to make a sweet bean paste for Asian desserts and are easier to digest than most beans.
* Mung beans are sprouted to make the bean sprouts used in stir-fries. They are also wonderful in dals or soups.

Long-Cooking Beans

COMMON BEANS, HEIRLOOM BEANS, AND TYPICAL SUBSTITUTIONS: *These cook in about 2 hours if soaked and as long as 4 hours if not soaked. They cook well in a slow cooker overnight or during the day (unsoaked beforehand), which is my favorite way to cook them.*

KIDNEY FAMILY: Boil these beans for a full 10 minutes on the stove before adding to the slow cooker or oven. This is because kidney beans contain a toxic agent, phytohaemagglutinin, also known as kidney bean lectin, that can only be destroyed if brought up to a boiling temperature. This step is not necessary for other types of dried beans and has already been done for you in canned kidney beans.

* **Red kidney beans** are the ones most thought of as kidney beans and hold up well enough to be used in salads, but will cook down with a little extra effort.
* **White kidneys or cannellini beans** contain about 30 percent less phytohaemagglutinin but should still be boiled as a best practice for food safety.

- **Flageolet beans** are immature white kidneys that cook in about one hour and are used in cassoulets and other French dishes. They do not need to be boiled, and have a creamy texture when cooked down.
- **Small red beans** are not in the kidney family but are traditionally used in New Orleans–style red beans and rice, as well as Nicaraguan and other Latino cuisines. Unlike red kidney beans, they do not need to be boiled for 10 minutes before cooking.

PINTOS AND HEIRLOOM SUBSTITUTIONS: These beans become softer the longer they cook and are perfect for making a nice thick stew, plain beans, or refried beans. In fact, they are great in anything that doesn't require a very firm bean.

- **Pinto beans** are a tasty, inexpensive bean that can be cooked down to make its own gravy or, even better, into refried beans.
- **Rattlesnake beans** are beautifully marked and sometimes known as the preacher bean.
- **Anasazi beans** are a bit easier to digest and have a bolder flavor than pintos.
- **Appaloosa beans** have markings similar to those of Appaloosa ponies and can take the place of pintos or black beans.
- **Borlotti beans** (also known as cranberry beans) are the hearty beans that make such tasty gravy that they almost single-handedly made heirloom beans popular.
- **Tiger's Eye beans** are tasty beans that become very soft when cooked and make good refried beans.
- **Rio Zape beans** have hints of chocolate and are great cooked plain.
- **Vaquero beans** are black and white and a relative of the anasazi bean.

BLACK BEAN VARIETIES: These beans come in different sizes and shapes, and some even have patterns. You can use any of them when your recipe calls for black beans. It's a great place to start playing with new-to-you varieties.

- **Black turtle beans** are traditional black beans used in different cuisines.
- **Black Calypso beans** are great in soups and stews and have the flavor of a potato.
- **Black Valentine beans**, or **Midnight beans**, are similar to kidney beans but can be used like any other black bean.
- **Ayocote negro (black runner beans)** are larger black beans that are a great star of any dish—they are among my favorite beans!

WHITE BEANS: These are different from one another, yet interchangeable in most recipes.

- **Cannellini beans** are white kidney beans that are fairly firm.
- **Marrow beans** have a creamy texture.
- **Navy** and **Great Northern beans** are dense and can be used for baked beans, cassoulet, and more.

BEANS WITH INTERESTING SHAPES: These beans are among my favorites. Although each bean tastes slightly different, I find that the mouthfeel of these really sets them apart.

- **Ayocote negro** are large and toothsome and make a great focal point in a dish.
- **Goat's Eye beans** are football-shaped and best cooked plain because they taste great all by themselves.
- **Good Mother Stallard beans** are also football-shaped with a great mouthfeel and make a perfect pot liquor.

OTHER BEANS: From chestnut-flavored Christmas lima beans to uniquely-shaped and firm garbanzo beans, this category is full of interesting beans to add into your meals. There are beans of all sizes and cooking times, so there's plenty to pick from!

- **Lima beans** are large, have fairly thick skins, and are great when cooked in the oven with veggies.
- **Christmas limas** are a large, colorful lima with a chestnut flavor.
- **Fava beans** are available fresh, dried, and frozen. I like to use frozen because you can have them anytime of the year and you can use them as-is.
  - Fresh fava beans are packed better than any other bean. There is the outer pod that you shell before cooking. Then, after you've removed the beans, you boil them for about 2 minutes and rinse them under cool water. Finally, you remove the outer skin of each bean to get to the part that you'll use. (Not an easy process, but fresh fava bean lovers feel that it's worth the time and effort.)
  - Dried favas also have this outer skin in their whole dried form but are removed in the split form, so choose according to how much work you're willing to do.

– The frozen ones can be just thrown into dishes like the risottos on pages 154-155.

* **Tepary beans** are native to the New World and are smallish beans, just larger than a lentil. They come in brown or white and grow well in drought conditions. They were a staple in Native American cuisine. While small, these beans take just as long to cook as larger beans.

* **Chickpeas** are different from all the other beans. They have a nutty flavor and hold their shape against everything except a food processor. These are the best stand-ins for seitan or tofu and make a great meat substitute. At Indian markets, you can get black and green chickpeas, and you can use these in any recipes that call for regular chickpeas.

* **Soybeans** are the longest cooking bean, and you should always buy organic to ensure that they are not genetically modified. I recommend that you soak these because of the long cooking time, and be mindful that you cook them all the way.

HOW TO MODIFY RECIPES FOR YOUR SPECIAL DIET

I've done my best to make recipe options so they can fit into almost anyone's diet. This book has nutritional information that you can use as a guideline, but if you have a medical condition, please do the numbers in your normal nutritional program as well. The numbers will vary depending on the type of nondairy milk you use and whether it's unsweetened or not. Also, there are many modifications you can choose, so please take that into account when calculating the nutritional information of your finished dish.

I do not list sodium in the nutritional information because 90 percent of the time I tell you to salt to taste. This allows people with high blood pressure to use less, and people who prefer a ton of salt to use more. I use less when cooking and have salt on the table for guests. The longer I eat with less salt in my diet, the more I seem to appreciate the taste of other foods, so hang in there if your doctor has asked you to cut down on sodium.

Nut Allergies

There are nuts in some of the recipes. If the recipe includes Cashew Cream (page 28), you can substitute Extra-Thick Silken Tofu Sour Cream (page 28) or use store-bought vegan sour cream or vegan unsweetened yogurt instead.

Some of the cheezy spread recipes call for nuts to make a creamier texture. You can substitute silken tofu to get similar results.

Gluten-free

Almost all the recipes in this book have gluten-free alternatives. I am not gluten-free, but I relied on quite a few gluten-free recipe testers so that they could point out alternatives and subsitutions to include in the final recipes.

Recipes involving wheat-based seitan will not be for you, but other recipes, including two kinds of vegan sausage, are waiting for you to try them. (There are non-seitan alternatives in most of the recipes as well.) Be sure to try Monika Soria Caruso's custom gluten-free baking blend in the recipe Monika's Gluten-Free Biscuits (page 25). You might find that you like it more than your normal gluten-free blend.

I do my best to point out which ingredients you need to check for gluten, but please don't limit yourself to only checking those.

Soy-free

Most of the recipes are soy-free or at the very least have soy-free options in them. Recipes calling for edamame or black soybeans can easily be switched out for your favorite bean. Good Mother Stallard, kidney beans, chickpeas, and other cooked beans that retain their shape and don't get too mushy will work great.

In the few recipes that call for tempeh and tofu, most of them allow you to leave the soy out and advise you to add extra beans in their place.

No-Added-Oil Diets

The no-added-oil lifestyle encouraged by the *The Engine 2 Diet*, Joel Fuhrman, M.D., John McDougall, M.D., and Caldwell Esselstyn, M.D., has gained quite a following. My recipes are already low in fat and most can be made with no added oil with a few simple modifications.

Please note that although the words "oil-free" and "oil-free options" are being used throughout the book, there may be nuts, avocados, and other higher fat foods that may or may not fit into your particular diet. Feel free to make substitutions as needed and reference Susan Voisin's site, Fatfree Vegan Recipes (www.fatfreevegan.com), for more ideas on modifications.

One option in the recipes is not sautéing veggies in olive oil. Instead, heat a small amount of water or veggie broth to cook them in. The other option is to find an alternative to greasing baking pans. Cookie sheets, pie pans, and so on can be lined with baking parchment paper or silicone mats or molds.

STAPLES: RECIPES TO KEEP YOUR FOOD BUDGET IN CHECK

I'm always looking for a way to cut my food costs. The more I save, the more I can splurge on heirloom beans, spices, and other things I can't make myself.

You will use the following staple recipes in other recipes in the book, but you can also use them in your own favorite recipes. Making things from scratch means you have control over all the ingredients, and you can change up the spices and some of the ingredients to suit you or what's in your pantry.

On the other hand, if time is more important to you, store-bought alternatives will also work in the recipes in this book.

Savory Golden Bouillon

▶ SOY-FREE ▶ GLUTEN-FREE ▶ OIL-FREE

This is the only recipe I'm including from my first book, *The Vegan Slow Cooker*. I changed the name here from its original Chickeny Bouillon and added the option to make it on the stove top. But other than that, it's the bold bouillon you know and love.

1 large onion, cut into quarters

2 medium carrots, chopped (peeled if not organic)

½ cup (120 ml) water

2 sprigs fresh thyme or 1 teaspoon dried

2 stalks celery, chopped

2 sprigs fresh parsley or 1 teaspoon dried

½ teaspoon pepper or to taste

1 teaspoon salt (optional)

½ cup (48 g) nutritional yeast

YIELD: 1½ to 2 cups (355 to 475 ml)

PER 2-TABLESPOON (28 ML) SERVING: 15.6 calories; 0.1 g total fat; 0 g saturated fat; 1.2 g protein; 2.7 g carbohydrate; 0.7 g dietary fiber; 0 mg cholesterol.

TOTAL PREP TIME: 10 minutes

TOTAL COOKING TIME: 20 to 30 minutes for stove top, 8 to 12 hours for slow cooker

STOVE-TOP DIRECTIONS

Add everything except the nutritional yeast to a covered saucepan. Cook over medium heat until the carrots are soft, about 20 to 30 minutes. Add more water if the ingredients get too dry during cooking and start to stick to the pan.

After cooking, remove the thyme stems. Add the contents of the pan and the nutritional yeast to a blender or food processor. Blend until smooth. Store and/or freeze according to the slow cooker directions.

SLOW COOKER DIRECTIONS

The night before: Cut the veggies and herbs and then store in the fridge.

In the morning: Add everything except the nutritional yeast to the slow cooker. Cook on low for 8 to 12 hours. Don't worry about coming home on time because you can cook this as much as 12 hours and it will still come out great. The water will keep the veggies from sticking to the crock, but you can spray the empty crock with oil before adding your ingredients for extra security.

After cooking, remove the thyme stems. Add the contents of the crock and the nutritional yeast to a blender or food processor. If using a blender, always be sure to purée in small batches of about 2 to 3 cups at a time. If it's too full, the hot liquid might push the lid off. You can also use an immersion blender if you want, but the texture won't be quite as smooth.

Store in the refrigerator for about a week and/or freeze in ice cube trays using 2 tablespoons (28 ml) of bouillon per cube. I typically use 1 to 2 tablespoons (14 to 28 ml) of store-bought bouillon when a recipe calls for 1 veggie bouillon cube, so that works out to 2 to 4 tablespoons (28 to 56) of this recipe or about 1 to 2 ice cubes. (The average ice cube tray holds about 2 tablespoons [28 ml].)

Easy Veggie Bouillon

▶ SOY-FREE ▶ GLUTEN-FREE ▶ OIL-FREE

I hate buying liquid broth or bouillon because it's expensive, is in wasteful packaging, and has too much salt. This recipe freezes great, so you can have some on hand whenever you need it. This is a great bouillon to make if you're not a big fan of nutritional yeast, and you can use it wherever bouillon is called for in this book or your own recipes.

1 medium onion, chopped

4 medium carrots, chopped (peeled if not organic)

5 stalks celery, chopped

½ cup (35 g) sliced mushrooms

1 cup (235 ml) water

½ teaspoon ground rosemary or 2 teaspoons fresh

½ cup (30 g) fresh parsley

Salt, to taste

Other fresh herbs (optional)

:::

YIELD: 3 to 4 cups (700 to 950 g)

PER 2-TABLESPOON (28 ML) SERVING: 7.3 calories; 0 g total fat; 0 g saturated fat; 0.3 g protein; 1.6 g carbohydrate; 0.5 g dietary fiber; 0 mg cholesterol.

TOTAL PREP TIME: 20 minutes

TOTAL COOKING TIME: 45 minutes for oven, 20 minutes for stove top

Cook the veggies either in the oven or on the stove (see below).

OVEN DIRECTIONS
Preheat the oven to 350°F (180°C, or gas mark 4). Add the onion, carrots, celery, mushrooms, and water to a Dutch oven or other covered oven-safe dish and cook until the veggies are soft and the onions are translucent. This will take about 45 minutes. Remove from the heat and let cool.

STOVE-TOP DIRECTIONS
Add the onion, carrots, celery, mushrooms, and water to a pan and cook over medium heat until the veggies are soft and the onions are translucent. This will take about 20 minutes. Remove from the heat and let cool.

To proceed, add the cool mixture to a blender or food processor and blend until smooth. Add the rosemary and parsley, then blend again. Add salt, if desired.

Serving Suggestions & Variations

You can customize the bouillon with your favorite herbs to tailor it to the dishes you are going to make. Freeze the bullion in ice cube trays and then transfer the frozen cubes to a resealable bag in the freezer so they are always on hand. When a recipe calls for 1 veggie bouillon cube, you can use about 1 to 2 ice cubes of this bouillon instead. (The average ice cube holds about 2 tablespoons [28 ml].)

Simple Pantry Salsa

▶ SOY-FREE ▶ GLUTEN-FREE ▶ OIL-FREE

Sometimes you need some salsa fast and don't want to or can't go to the store. Maybe you're already cozy in the house or it's storming outside. Don't panic—just grab a few cans of tomatoes from your pantry (or frozen salsa you've put up earlier).

2 cans (14.5 ounces, or 410 g each) diced tomatoes or 3 cups (540 g) fresh

1 can (4 ounces, or 115 g) green chiles

2 cloves garlic, minced

1 or 2 chipotles in adobo sauce, to taste (optional)

Salt, to taste

Add-ins such as fresh chopped onion, fresh chopped cilantro, diced jalapeños, chili powder, or ground cumin (optional)

Combine all the ingredients in a food processor along with any of the extras you'd like to add. Blend until it's as chunky or smooth as you like it. You can freeze leftovers!

YIELD: 3½ cups (910 g)

PER ½-CUP (130 G) SERVING: 25.8 calories; 0.1 g total fat; 0 g saturated fat; 1.1 g protein; 6.1 g carbohydrate; 0.9 g dietary fiber; 0 mg cholesterol.

TOTAL PREP TIME: 10 minutes

Baked Crispy Chickpea Seitan Patties

▶ SOY-FREE* ▶ OIL-FREE OPTION**

Cheryl, my picky eater, loves the crispy vegan chicken patties you can get in the frozen food section. Unfortunately, they have a few ingredients that I'd rather avoid. Plus, many brands change back and forth from being vegan to not being vegan anymore. This is my healthy and much cheaper alternative. These are particularly tasty with the cornbread waffles and gravy on page 102, and awesome in lemon sauce.

1½ cups (246 g) cooked chickpeas or 1 can (15 ounces, or 425 g), rinsed and drained

¼ cup (24 g) nutritional yeast

1 teaspoon dried thyme or 1 tablespoon (2.4 g) fresh

½ teaspoon salt

¼ teaspoon black pepper

¼ teaspoon garlic powder or 1 clove garlic, minced

⅛ teaspoon ground rosemary

½ cup (120 ml) unsweetened nondairy milk (*use soy-free)

1 cup (120 g) vital wheat gluten flour

2 to 3 cups (224 to 336 g) bread crumbs, for coating (I like to use whole wheat panko)

:::

YIELD: 10 patties

PER PATTY: 151.8 calories; 1.1 g total fat; 0.3 g saturated fat; 14.4 g protein; 21.0 g carbohydrate; 3.8 g dietary fiber; 0 mg cholesterol.

TOTAL PREP TIME: 20 minutes

TOTAL COOKING TIME: 20 minutes

Preheat the oven to 350°F (180°C, or gas mark 4). Oil two cookie sheets **or line with parchment paper.

Add everything except the wheat gluten flour and bread crumbs to a food processor and purée. Add ⅔ cup (80 g) of the gluten flour and process until combined. Then process a minute or two more, letting the food processor do the kneading for you.

Put the mixture on a cutting board. Knead in the remaining ⅓ cup (40 g) wheat gluten.

Cut the dough into 10 pieces, roll into little balls, and press into patties between your hands. You want to make the patties thinner than your desired end result because they will puff up some during baking. Spread the bread crumbs on a plate, press the patties into the crumbs, and then turn and press on the other side. The dough should still be wet enough for the bread crumbs to stick.

Place the breaded patties on the sheet pan. Bake for 15 minutes. Flip them over using a wide spatula and bake for 5 to 10 minutes more.

Serving Suggestions & Variations

• Shape the dough into stars, strips, nuggets, or other shapes before coating.

• These freeze well, so make a double batch and enjoy them for a few effortless meals. They're great reheated in the oven or in a sauté pan. Add vegan cheese and marinara sauce, put them in sandwiches, or use them to veganize some of your old favorite recipes.

Bean Chorizo Crumbles

▶ SOY-FREE ▶ GLUTEN-FREE ▶ OIL-FREE

Most people can buy soy chorizo in the store, but people who need to eat soy-free or like to make everything from scratch need an alternative. This recipe is a bean- and grain-based solution that's just as tasty with no added fat. You can vary the bean and grains to suit what's in your pantry.

2 tablespoons (15 g) ancho chili powder

1 tablespoon (7.5 g) pastilla chili powder

1 tablespoon (3 g) oregano

1 teaspoon ground cumin

1 teaspoon salt

½ teaspoon pepper

3 cloves garlic, minced, or 1 teaspoon garlic powder

1½ cups (270 g) cooked white beans or 1 can (15 ounces, or 425 g), rinsed and drained

2 teaspoons apple cider vinegar

4 cups (about 740 g) cooked grains (I like to use a combination of quinoa and millet)

:::

YIELD: 6 cups (660 g)

PER ½-CUP (110 G) SERVING: 85.7 calories; 0.8 g total fat; 0 g saturated fat; 3.6 g protein; 17.1 g carbohydrate; 2.3 g dietary fiber; 0 mg cholesterol.

TOTAL PREP TIME: 15 minutes

TOTAL COOKING TIME: 15 minutes

Heat a sauté pan over medium heat and add the spices, salt, and pepper. Stir constantly until the spices are lightly toasted, about 3 to 4 minutes. Add the garlic and sauté for about 2 minutes more.

Pour the toasted spices into a large mixing bowl and add the beans. Mash the beans and the spices together until there are no whole beans left.

Add the vinegar and cooked grains. Mix while mashing any whole beans that may have snuck through.

Heat a large nonstick sauté pan over medium-high heat. The mixture is the same texture as Lightlife's Gimme Lean or an extremely wet dough. Make a thin layer of the chorizo in the pan, chopping with a spatula and sautéing until it looks "crumbled." Turn out the cooked mixture onto a plate or cookie sheet to cool.

Add more of the wet chorizo to the pan and keep cooking it in batches until it is all cooked crumbles. Use as you would store-bought vegan chorizo. This makes enough chorizo for three or four meals and freezes great.

Serving Suggestions & Variations

Substitute any chili powders you have on hand if you don't have the ones called for here.

Black Bean Breakfast Sausage Patties

▶ SOY-FREE ▶ GLUTEN-FREE OPTION* ▶ OIL-FREE OPTION**

These sausage patties are also nut-free per a request from a reader. I love the texture from the cooked grain and you get a sausagelike color from the black beans.

⅓ cup (67 g) millet

⅓ cup (69 g) amaranth

⅓ cup (58 g) quinoa, rinsed well

2½ cups (570 ml) water

1 teaspoon Savory Golden Bouillon (page 19)

1½ cups (258 g) cooked black beans or 1 can (15 ounces, or 425 g), rinsed and drained

½ cup (48 g) rolled oats (*make sure they are marked gluten-free)

¼ to ½ cup (60 to 120 ml) water

2 tablespoons (14 g) ground flaxseed mixed with ¼ cup (60 ml) warm water

1 teaspoon sage

1½ teaspoons marjoram

1½ teaspoons oregano

1 teaspoon ground rosemary

1 teaspoon smoked paprika

½ teaspoon ground coriander

½ teaspoon granulated garlic

½ teaspoon onion powder (optional)

Salt and pepper, to taste (try it with smoked salt)

::

YIELD: 42 small patties

PER TWO-PATTY SERVING: 58.6 calories; 0.7 g total fat; 0.1 g saturated fat; 2.4 g protein; 8.4 g carbohydrate; 1.6 g dietary fiber; 0 mg cholesterol.

TOTAL PREP TIME: 20 minutes

TOTAL COOKING TIME: 20 minutes to cook grains and 35 minutes to bake patties

Preheat the oven to 350°F (180°C, or gas mark 4). Oil 2 cookie sheets **or line with parchment paper.

Combine the millet, amaranth, quinoa, water, and bouillon in a saucepan and bring to a boil. Decrease the heat to low, cover, and cook until the grains are completely cooked, about 20 to 25 minutes.

Meanwhile, add the beans, oats, and water to a food processor and purée. Transfer to a large mixing bowl and add the flaxseed mixture.

Add the cooked grains to the bean mixture along with all the herbs and spices. Mix thoroughly, taste, and then add salt and pepper to taste.

Using a small cookie scoop that holds about 1½ tablespoons (22.5 g), put the mixture on the cookie sheet and then use your hand to flatten the patties. (If the mixture sticks to your hand try keeping your hands damp with water.)

Cook for 25 minutes and then gently flip the patties and cook for 10 to 15 minutes more.

These freeze well, so don't worry that this recipe makes quite a few.

Serving Suggestions & Variations

• These are great served alongside pancakes and waffles. Be sure to try them crumbled in a tofu scramble or pasta sauce.

• Try these crumbled with Southern-Style White Bean Gravy (page 41) over my Basic Whole Wheat Biscuits (page 26) or Monika's Gluten-Free Biscuits (page 25).

• These are great on their own, but are not good to use in stews if you want them to remain patties. When added to a sauce, they revert back to their original form as grains.

Monika's Gluten-Free Biscuits

▶ GLUTEN-FREE ▶ SOY-FREE OPTION*

This recipe is kindly provided by my friend Monika Soria Caruso of www.windycityvegan.wordpress.com. She's a wonderful gluten-free baker and even has her own flour blend. If you don't want to make the custom flour and starch blend in this recipe, you can use 2 cups plus 2 tablespoons (285 g) pre-mixed gluten-free flour blend, plus extra for kneading, in place of the sorghum flour, millet flour, potato starch, and tapioca flour.

¾ cup (100 g) sweet sorghum flour, plus extra for kneading

¾ cup (90 g) millet flour

Scant ¼ cup (48 g) potato starch

6 tablespoons (45 g) tapioca flour or starch

2 teaspoons fine-grain sea salt

1 tablespoon (13.8 g) baking powder

½ cup (112 g) vegan shortening (such as one Earth Balance buttery margarine stick), chilled and cut into small cubes (*use soy free)

1 to 1 ⅓ cups (230 to 307 g) plain soy yogurt (*use coconut yogurt)

::

YIELD: 12 to 16 biscuits

PER BISCUIT: 166.8 calories; 8.2 g total fat; 2.3 g saturated fat; 2.4 g protein; 21.0 g carbohydrate; 1.0 g dietary fiber; 0 mg cholesterol.

TOTAL PREP TIME: 45 minutes

TOTAL COOKING TIME: 20 to 25 minutes

Sift the flours, starches, salt, and baking powder thoroughly in a large bowl and then transfer to a food processor. Distribute the cubes of chilled shortening evenly over the surface of the flour and pulse several times until the pieces of shortening are the size of peas.

Add 1 cup (230 g) of the yogurt and pulse just until incorporated. The dough will be stiff, with a few dry spots. If needed, add the remaining ⅓ cup (77 g) yogurt and pulse to incorporate. Transfer the dough to a large bowl, cover, and chill for half an hour.

Preheat the oven to 450°F (230°C, or gas mark 8) and place a cookie sheet on the center rack to preheat at the same time.

Tear a large piece of parchment paper the size of your cookie sheet. Lay it out flat and sprinkle lightly with gluten-free flour. Turn your dough out onto the parchment paper and sprinkle the top lightly with more flour so your fingers don't stick.

Pat the dough out into a 1-inch (2.5 cm) rectangle, cut in half, and stack one half onto the other. Repeat five or six times, patting the final rectangle to ½ to ¾ inch (1.3 to 2 cm) tall.

Cut the rectangle into several small pieces (about 12 to 16). Space them out as much as you can over the piece of parchment paper. Using a peel or another baking sheet, carefully transfer the parchment paper onto the preheated cookie sheet. Bake for 20 to 25 minutes until the biscuits have turned golden.

These keep for up to 2 days if wrapped loosely in a dish towel, but taste best if eaten the same day.

Basic Whole Wheat Biscuits

▶ SOY-FREE OPTION*

The problem with whole wheat flour in biscuits is that it makes them denser. Try my little trick and yours will be lighter. Granted, not as light as if you used Martha White flour, but these are also much better for you.

1 cup (120 g) white whole wheat flour

1 cup (120 g) whole wheat pastry flour

1 tablespoon baking powder

½ teaspoon salt

¼ teaspoon baking soda

½ cup (112 g) vegan margarine or shortening (shortening is best) (*use soy-free)

¾ cup (175 ml) unsweetened coconut milk or other unsweetened nondairy milk (*use soy-free)

....

YIELD: 8 large biscuits

PER BISCUIT: 249.7 calories; 15.0 g total fat; 5.5 g saturated fat; 3.6 g protein; 23.6 g carbohydrate; 4.0 g dietary fiber; 0 mg cholesterol.

TOTAL PREP TIME: 20 minutes

TOTAL COOKING TIME: 15 to 20 minutes

Preheat the oven to 400°F (200°C, or gas mark 6) and oil a baking sheet.

In a food processor, add the flours and process for about 2 minutes. This makes the flour a little finer. Add the baking powder, salt, and baking soda. Process until mixed thoroughly.

If you are using stick shortening, cut into small pieces; if you are getting it out of a tub, measure the ½ cup (112 g) and then drop it in ½ teaspoons. Add the shortening little by little through the food processor tube until you've used it all and the mixture looks like coarse cornmeal. Pour this mixture into a mixing bowl, add the milk, and mix with a wooden spoon until you need to use your hands and then dig in!

Dump the mixture out on a floured cutting board. You want to get some good layers in your biscuits, so roll the dough out with a rolling pin and fold it in half. Roll it out again, fold it into quarters, and then roll it out to about a ½-inch (1.3 cm) thickness.

Use a 1-quart (1 L) wide-mouth canning jar, a large drinking glass, or about a 3-inch (7.5 cm) round cookie cutter to cut out the biscuits. Once you've cut out about 4 you will have run out of room to cut more, so ball up the remaining dough, roll out again to ½-inch (1.3-cm) thickness, and cut more. You should get about 8 large biscuits. There will almost always be some dough left over that can't make one more large biscuit. I shape that small piece of dough about the same thickness and cook it near the center of the cookie sheet. It's the dog's treat for staying out of my way while I'm baking.

Bake for 15 to 20 minutes or until firm to the touch (but not hard).

Sweet Red Bean Paste

▶ SOY-FREE ▶ GLUTEN-FREE ▶ OIL-FREE

This sweet bean paste is used in many Asian desserts and in a few in this book, too. Before I made it, I figured it would have exotic ingredients, but I was wrong. You probably already have what you need in your pantry right now. Once you make your first batch, try it out in the Red Bean–Filled Mini Muffins on page 46.

1 cup (197 g) dry adzuki beans

3 cups (710 g) water

1 cup (200 g) sugar

Put the beans and water in a saucepan and bring to a boil. Decrease the heat to low, cover, and cook until the beans are soft, about 1 to 1½ hours.

Once the beans are done, add the sugar and stir to combine. You can keep cooking until the beans are thick, like the texture of miso. I like to leave a few bean chunks, but you can put it into the food processor if you'd like it smooth.

Store in the fridge for up to 1 week. You can also freeze the rest for another batch of goodies later.

YIELD: 3 cups (510 g)

PER 2-TABLESPOON (21 G) SERVING: 87.9 calories; 0.6 g total fat; 0 g saturated fat; 7.3 g protein; 13.2 g carbohydrate; 1.0 g dietary fiber; 5.0 mg cholesterol.

TOTAL PREP TIME: 5 minutes

TOTAL COOKING TIME: 1 to 1½ hours

Easy Almond Parm

▶ SOY-FREE ▶ GLUTEN-FREE ▶ OIL-FREE

This is a simple and inexpensive vegan Parmesan substitute. It goes great with the Baked Beany Mac and Cheezy on page 149.

½ cup (73 g) toasted, skinned almonds

¼ cup (29 g) nutritional yeast

½ teaspoon salt (smoked or plain)

Grind all the ingredients together in a food processor until the almond pieces are very small and granular. Store the leftovers in the fridge for up to a month.

YIELD: ¾ cup (74 g)

PER 1-TABLESPOON (6 G) SERVING: 32.9 calories; 2.1 g total fat; 0.2 g saturated fat; 2.2 g protein; 2.0 g carbohydrate; 1.1 g dietary fiber; 0 mg cholesterol.

TOTAL PREP TIME: 20 minutes

Vegan Sour Cream Alternatives

▶ GLUTEN-FREE ▶ OIL-FREE ▶ SOY-FREE (FOR CASHEW CREAM)

Some people love the convenience of store-bought vegan sour cream but don't like a few of the ingredients that are in some of them. Cashew Cream is a great soy-free solution, and the tofu-based one can be made super thick.

Cashew Cream

1 cup (140 g) cashews

¼ to ½ cup (60 to 120 ml) water

Juice of 1 lemon

Add the cashews, ¼ cup (60 ml) of the water, and the lemon juice to a food processor or blender and blend until smooth, scraping down the sides as you go. If you are using a food processor, it will take longer than you think to get a smooth mixture. It will not be quite as silky smooth as if you had used a powerful blender, but it will still taste great!

Add the remaining ¼ cup (60 ml) water if you need to thin the mixture or if you have a less powerful blender.

YIELD: 1¼ cups (285 g)

PER 2-TABLESPOON (29 G) SERVING: 49.2 calories; 5.2 g total fat; 1.0 g saturated fat; 2.0 g protein; 3.6 g carbohydrate; 0 g dietary fiber; 0 mg cholesterol.

TOTAL PREP TIME: 5 to 10 minutes

Extra-Thick Silken Tofu Sour Cream

1 package (12.3 ounces, or 350 g) silken tofu

1 to 3 tablespoons (15 to 45 ml) water

Juice of 1 lemon

Add the tofu, 1 tablespoon (15 ml) of the water, and the lemon juice to a food processor or blender and blend until smooth, scraping down the sides as you go.

Add the remaining 1 to 2 tablespoons (15 to 30 ml) water if you need to thin the mixture or if you have a less powerful blender.

YIELD: 1 cup (350 g)

PER 2-TABLESPOON (44 G) SERVING: 23.1 calories; 1.0 g total fat; 0 g saturated fat; 1.9 g protein; 1.0 g carbohydrate; 0 g dietary fiber; 0 mg cholesterol.

TOTAL PREP TIME: 5 minutes

Spice Blends

▶ SOY-FREE ▶ GLUTEN-FREE ▶ OIL-FREE

Save some money and make them taste just the way you like them by making your own spice blends.

Cajun Spice Blend

2 teaspoons paprika

2 teaspoons thyme

1 teaspoon oregano

1 teaspoon marjoram

1 bay leaf or ½ teaspoon ground bay leaf

½ teaspoon cayenne pepper

½ teaspoon onion powder

½ teaspoon granulated garlic powder

½ teaspoon lemon zest

¼ teaspoon black pepper

⅛ teaspoon allspice

⅛ teaspoon cloves

Grind everything together in a spice grinder or in a small food processor for about 10 minutes. If you are using a whole bay leaf, it's very important that it gets ground into a powder. If you don't have a spice grinder you can buy powdered bay leaf to use in this.

YIELD: 3 tablespoons (42 g)

TOTAL PREP TIME: 5 minutes

DIY Poultry Seasoning

2 tablespoons (4 g) ground sage

2 tablespoons (5.4 g) thyme

1 tablespoon (1.7 g) marjoram

2 teaspoons celery seed

Mix everything together and store in an airtight container.

YIELD: ⅓ cup (16 g)

TOTAL PREP TIME: 5 minutes

Serving Variation

Poultry Seasoning is a great spice blend to use with chickpeas. The combination of the two is perfect to use in recipes in place of tempeh or seitan. It's also a great way to veganize some of your favorite childhood dishes.

MORNING BEANS

Beany Breakfast and Brunch Dishes

Brunch is my favorite meal of the whole week. Saturday and Sunday are leisurely days and the perfect time to spend with friends. And there's nothing I like better than to feed my friends tasty treats. You may not think of beans when you think of brunch, but they are naturals. They help you cut down on fat in sweet treats and make them heartier at the same time.

Almost-a-Meal White Bean Pesto Muffins

▶ SOY-FREE OPTION* ▶ GLUTEN-FREE OPTION** ▶ OIL-FREE OPTION***

The basil in these muffins adds a nice burst of summer anytime of the year. These are a perfect portable meal and a great addition to your brunch table.

FOR THE DRY INGREDIENTS

2 cups (250 g) white whole wheat flour (**use gluten-free)

1 teaspoon baking powder

½ teaspoon baking soda

¼ teaspoon salt

FOR THE WET INGREDIENTS

1½ cups (269 g) cooked white beans or 1 can (15 ounces, or 425 g), rinsed and drained

1 cup (235 ml) nondairy milk (*use soy-free)

2 tablespoons (14 g) ground flaxseed mixed with ¼ cup (60 ml) warm water

2 tablespoons (28 ml) olive oil (***use water)

½ teaspoon oregano

¼ to ½ teaspoon red pepper flakes (optional, leave out for kids!)

¼ teaspoon ground rosemary

½ teaspoon black pepper

1 cup (24 g) fresh basil leaves

Preheat the oven to 350°F (180°C, or gas mark 4) and oil your muffin pans ***or line with paper liners.

To prepare the dry ingredients, combine all the ingredients in a large bowl. Set aside.

To prepare the wet ingredients, add all the ingredients to a food processor, except for the basil, and purée until smooth. Add the basil and pulse until the pieces of basil are tiny, but not puréed. (You want flecks of basil, not green muffins!)

Add the purée to the dry ingredients. Mix with a wooden spoon and fill the muffin tins with the mixture. Bake for 20 to 30 minutes or until a toothpick inserted into the center comes out clean.

Fancy Bean Substitutes: Hutterite, Cannellini, Vallarta

....

YIELD: 12 muffins

PER MUFFIN: 133.6 calories; 3.5 g total fat; 0.8 g saturated fat; 4.5 g protein; 21.3 g carbohydrate; 4.5 g dietary fiber; 0 mg cholesterol.

TOTAL PREP TIME: 20 minutes

TOTAL COOKING TIME: 20 to 30 minutes

Almost-a-Meal Black Bean Tamale Muffins

▶ GLUTEN-FREE OPTION* ▶ SOY-FREE OPTION** ▶ OIL-FREE OPTION***

These hearty muffins are perfect for brunch, an on-the-go lunch, or hearty snack.

FOR THE DRY INGREDIENTS

1 cup (120 g) whole wheat pastry flour (*use gluten-free)

1 cup (140 g) cornmeal

2 tablespoons (28 g) Ener-G or (14 g) ground flaxseed

1 teaspoon baking powder

½ teaspoon baking soda

¼ teaspoon salt

FOR THE WET INGREDIENTS

1½ cups (355 ml) unsweetened nondairy milk (**use soy-free)

½ cup (130 g) salsa, store-bought or homemade (page 21)

¼ teaspoon ground cumin

¼ teaspoon chili powder

½ cup (58 g) nondairy cheese (**use Daiya Pepper Jack or other soy-free vegan cheese or omit)

1½ cups (258 g) cooked black beans or 1 can (15 ounces, or 425 g), rinsed and drained

....

YIELD: 12 muffins

NUTRITIONAL INFORMATION WITHOUT NONDAIRY CHEESE

PER MUFFIN: 136.7 calories; 0.9 g total fat; 0.5 g saturated fat; 4.6 g protein; 26.3 g carbohydrate; 3.7 g dietary fiber; 0 mg cholesterol.

TOTAL PREP TIME: 15 minutes

TOTAL COOKING TIME: 20 to 30 minutes

Preheat the oven to 350°F (180°C, or gas mark 4). Oil your muffin pan ***or line with paper liners.

To prepare the dry ingredients, combine all the ingredients in a large bowl. Set aside.

To prepare the wet ingredients, add all the ingredients to a food processor and purée. (Although the nondairy cheese is not a liquid, it incorporates into the muffin better when chopped up in the food processor.)

Add the purée along with the beans to the dry ingredients and mix with a wooden spoon until incorporated. Fill the muffin tins with the mixture.

Bake for 20 to 30 minutes or until a toothpick inserted into the center comes out clean.

Fancy Bean Substitutes: Ayocote Negro, Black Valentine Beans, Sangre de Toro

Serving Suggestions & Variations

You can vary the flavor by trying different salsas or even adding sautéed seasonal veggies. The base flavor of the cornmeal will still shine through all your additions.

Lemon Coconut Chickpea Muffins

▶ SOY-FREE OPTION* ▶ GLUTEN-FREE OPTION** ▶ OIL-FREE OPTION***

I love the way the lemon brightens up these muffins and the coconut balances out the flavor perfectly. Try making large muffins instead of mini ones or even a loaf.

FOR THE DRY INGREDIENTS

1½ cups (180 g) whole wheat pastry flour (**use gluten-free)

½ cup (43 g) grated unsweetened coconut

1 teaspoon baking powder

½ teaspoon baking soda

¼ teaspoon salt

FOR THE WET INGREDIENTS

¾ cup (240 g) agave nectar

1 tablespoon (14 g) ground flaxseed mixed with 2 tablespoons (28 ml) warm water

1½ cups (246 g) cooked chickpeas or 1 can (15 ounces, or 425 g), rinsed and drained

1 cup (235 ml) nondairy milk (*use soy-free)

1 tablespoon (28 ml) lemon juice

1 tablespoon (6 g) lemon zest

1 teaspoon lemon extract

Preheat the oven to 350°F (180°C, or gas mark 4) and oil three (12-muffin) mini muffin pans ***or line with paper liners.

To prepare the dry ingredients, mix all the ingredients in a large bowl. Set aside.

To prepare the wet ingredients, add all the ingredients to a food processor and purée. Add the purée to the dry ingredients. Mix with a wooden spoon until combined. Fill the muffin tins with the mixture. Bake for 12 to 15 minutes or until a toothpick inserted into the center comes out clean.

YIELD: 36 mini muffins

PER MINI MUFFIN: 60.3 calories; 1.2 g total fat; 0.2 g saturated fat; 1.2 g protein; 11.5 g carbohydrate; 1.4 g dietary fiber; 0 mg cholesterol.

TOTAL PREP TIME: 15 minutes

TOTAL COOKING TIME: 12 to 15 minutes

Weekend Vanilla Belgian Waffles

▶ SOY-FREE OPTION* ▶ OIL-FREE

I love waffles, and going out for them was something I missed once I went vegan. That all changed once I bought my Belgian waffle maker. Now every weekend morning is another opportunity to make my own waffles. This batter has whole-grain flours, a bright vanilla flavor, and no added fat. The beans lend more nutrition than they do flavor, so you're fine to use less expensive white beans. Also, you can fool your bean-hating friends with them like I do!

FOR THE DRY INGREDIENTS

1½ cups (180 g) white whole wheat flour

¼ cup (40 g) brown rice flour

1 teaspoon baking powder

½ teaspoon baking soda

¼ teaspoon salt

½ teaspoon cinnamon

FOR THE WET INGREDIENTS

1½ cups (269 g) cooked white beans or 1 can (15 ounces, or 425 g), rinsed and drained

2½ cups (570 ml) unsweetened nondairy milk (*use soy-free)

1 tablespoon (14 g) ground flaxseed mixed with 2 tablespoons (28 ml) warm water

1 tablespoon (13 g) sugar

1½ teaspoons vanilla extract

Preheat the waffle iron.

To prepare the dry ingredients, sift all the ingredients into a large mixing bowl. Set aside.

To prepare the wet ingredients, add all the ingredients to a food processor and blend until smooth. Add the wet ingredients to the dry ingredients and mix with a wooden spoon.

Add the amount of batter that your waffle iron manufacturer recommends and cook according to the instructions.

....

YIELD: 6 Belgian waffles

PER WAFFLE: 227.3 calories; 3.2 g total fat; 2.1 g saturated fat; 8.2 g protein; 34.9 g carbohydrate; 7.7 g dietary fiber; 0 mg cholesterol.

TOTAL PREP TIME: 20 minutes

TOTAL COOKING TIME: 10 minutes

Mini Baked Rancheros with Tofu Scramble Mix

▶ GLUTEN-FREE OPTION* ▶ OIL-FREE OPTION**

This is the easiest fancy brunch dish ever. It looks like you spent much more time than you did on it, so don't feel bad about asking guests to bring the sparkling wine and orange juice! The kala namak salt makes the tofu taste exactly like scrambled eggs, and it's colored with turmeric so it looks like scrambled eggs too.

Three 8-inch (20-cm) whole wheat tortillas, cut into quarters (*use gluten-free)

FOR THE TOFU SCRAMBLE

7 ounces (200 g) tofu or half the amount in a 16 ounce (455 g) container, drained and pressed for 20 minutes (up to overnight if you are a planner)

½ teaspoon kala namak salt

½ teaspoon turmeric

¼ teaspoon paprika (plain or smoked)

¾ cup (83 g) Bean Chorizo Crumbles (page 23) or store-bought vegan chorizo

¾ cup (about 195 g) of your favorite salsa (fire-roasted is my favorite)

Toppings such as vegan shredded cheese, vegan sour cream, and olives (optional)

::

YIELD: 12 servings, 7 ounces (200 g) tofu scramble

PER SERVING (DOES NOT INCLUDE OPTIONAL TOPPINGS): 59.3 calories; 2.3 g total fat; 0.3 g saturated fat; 4.1 g protein; 9.2 g carbohydrate; 1.2 g dietary fiber; 0 mg cholesterol.

TOTAL PREP TIME: 20 minutes

TOTAL COOKING TIME: 20 minutes

Preheat the oven to 350°F (180°C, or gas mark 4). Spray a muffin tin with oil **or line with paper liners. Press 1 tortilla piece into each muffin cup, completely covering the bottom of the tin. This will help it hold the filling. (The ends will stick up, making a decorative mini tortilla cup.) Bake the empty tortilla cups in the oven for 10 minutes or until they are starting to get crisp, but not very brown. (You will be cooking them for 10 more minutes after they're filled.)

Meanwhile, to make the tofu scramble, crumble the tofu into a bowl and mix in the spices until the tofu has taken on the yellow turmeric color.

Remove the tortillas from the oven and add 1 tablespoon (15 g) chorizo to each tortilla cup, then layer 1 tablespoon tofu (15 g) scramble, and then top that with 1 tablespoon (16 g) salsa. You can top with shredded cheese, olives, or other toppings before putting them back in the oven or simply have bowls of toppings at the table so people can customize their own.

Bake the filled cups for 10 more minutes or until heated through.

Serving Suggestions & Variations

Just leave out the tofu scramble to make this tasty dish soy-free. Your guests will still love it!

Sausage-Spiced Savory Pancakes

▶ SOY-FREE OPTION* ▶ OIL-FREE ▶ GLUTEN-FREE OPTION**

The perfect marriage of sausage and pancakes, all in one small bite.

FOR THE DRY INGREDIENTS

½ cup (55 g) pecans, minced

1 cup (120 g) whole wheat pastry flour
(**use gluten-free)

2 tablespoons (12 g) nutritional yeast

1 tablespoon (2 g) sage

1 teaspoon baking powder

1 teaspoon thyme

1 teaspoon oregano

1 teaspoon paprika

½ teaspoon baking soda

½ teaspoon salt

FOR THE WET INGREDIENTS

1½ cups (269 g) cooked white beans or
1 can (15 ounces, or 425 g), rinsed and
drained

1 tablespoon (14 g) ground flaxseed
mixed with 2 tablespoons (28 ml)
warm water

1½ cups (355 ml) unsweetened
nondairy milk (*use soy-free)

....

YIELD: 36 mini pancakes

PER PANCAKE: 38.3 calories; 1.6 g total fat;
0.32 g saturated fat; 1.5 g protein; 5.0 g
carbohydrate; 1.4 g dietary fiber; 0 mg
cholesterol.

TOTAL PREP TIME: 20 minutes

TOTAL COOKING TIME: 10 minutes

To prepare the dry ingredients, mix all the ingredients in a large bowl. Set aside.

To prepare the wet ingredients, add all the ingredients to a food processor and purée. Add the purée to the dry ingredients. Mix with a wooden spoon until thoroughly combined.

Heat a nonstick skillet over medium heat and add about 1 tablespoon (15 g) of batter per pancake. Cook a few at a time, but avoid crowding them in the pan. Cook until you see a few bubbles on the top and the pancakes are dry around the edges, then flip and cook a few minutes more. Top with Maple Cashew Cream and/or plain maple syrup.

Maple Cashew Cream

▶ SOY-FREE ▶ GLUTEN-FREE ▶ OIL-FREE

1 cup (140 g) cashews

½ cup (120 ml) water

Juice of 1 lemon

1 tablespoon (20 g) maple syrup

1 tablespoon (15 ml) maple balsamic vinegar,
or more plain maple syrup

Add all of the ingredients to a blender and blend until smooth, scraping down the sides as you go.

....

YIELD: 1½ cups (350 g)

PER 2-TABLESPOON (29 G) SERVING: 106.8 calories; 8.0 g total fat; 1.3 g saturated fat; 3.3 g protein; 7.2 g carbohydrate; 0.4 g dietary fiber; 0 mg cholesterol.

TOTAL PREP TIME: 5 minutes

Roasted Root Veggie and Kidney Bean Hash

▶ SOY-FREE ▶ GLUTEN-FREE OPTION* ▶ OIL-FREE OPTION**

This is the kind of breakfast meal that also fits in perfectly at the dinner table. Leftovers make a great lunch during the week.

2 tablespoons (28 ml) olive oil (**use water or broth)

½ onion, minced

2 cloves garlic, minced

4 to 5 cups (about 610 g) roasted root veggies (see below for roasting instructions)

3 cups (531 g) cooked kidney beans or 2 cans (15 ounces, or 425 g each), rinsed and drained

1 teaspoon Dijon mustard

1 to 2 teaspoons ketchup (*use gluten-free) or tomato paste

½ to 1 teaspoon smoked or plain salt

Black pepper, to taste

::

YIELD: 4 servings

PER SCANT 2-CUP (455 G) SERVING: 303.4 calories; 8.1 g total fat; 1.1 g saturated fat; 14.0 g protein; 42.3 g carbohydrate; 13.6 g dietary fiber; 0 mg cholesterol.

TOTAL PREP TIME: 70 minutes (includes roasting veggies in the oven)

TOTAL COOKING TIME: 20 minutes

Heat the oil in a large sauté pan over medium heat. Add the onion and sauté until translucent, about 5 minutes. Add the garlic and sauté for 1 more minute.

Add the roasted veggies and kidney beans and cook until they are heated through, about 15 minutes. Then add the mustard, ketchup, and salt and mix well. Season with pepper to taste.

This would be a great brunch side with scrambled tofu. You can add in some chopped seitan or Gardein beef-less tips to make it heartier, and then you can feed those drop-in guests at your next brunch!

ROASTED VEGGIES INSTRUCTIONS:
Roasting can really bring out beautiful tastes in not-so-beautiful veggies. Radishes are no longer too strong, but mellow and almost buttery. I love using parsnips, rutabagas, sunchokes, celery root, and potatoes. You can also roast asparagus and other more delicate veggies, but check those often because they cook so much quicker than root veggies. You can cook root veggies and delicate veggies together by cutting the longer-cooking veggies very small and leaving the quick-cooking ones large or even whole.

I tried roasting in the oven two different ways: one covered with aluminum foil and one not covered. I cooked both at 375°F (190°C, or gas mark 5) for about 40 minutes and stirred them halfway. I found the one that I covered (until the last 10 or 15 minutes of cooking) to be juicy and lush. I liked the uncovered ones, but the texture was a little tougher and they took a little longer to cook.

Fancy Bean Substitutes: Sangre de Toro, Bolita, Lila

Southern-Style White Bean Gravy

▶ SOY-FREE OPTION* ▶ GLUTEN-FREE
▶ OIL-FREE

This is the easiest gravy ever. The beans thicken it so you don't have to bother with a roux. Why yes, it is oil-free!

1½ cups (269 g) cooked white beans or 1 can (15 ounces, or 425 g), rinsed and drained

¾ cup (175 ml) unsweetened nondairy milk (*use soy-free)

¼ teaspoon salt

¼ to ½ teaspoon black pepper

Combine all the ingredients in a food processor and blend until smooth. Taste and add more pepper if it doesn't pack a kick. Southern gravy is traditionally on the spicy side, but it's just from ground black pepper.

Transfer to a saucepan and warm over low heat and then serve over homemade biscuits split in half.

....

YIELD: 2 cups (470 ml)

PER ½-CUP (120 ML) SERVING: 77.1 calories; 0.9 g total fat; 0.9 g saturated fat; 4.7 g protein; 14.4 g carbohydrate; 4.5 g dietary fiber; 0 mg cholesterol.

TOTAL PREP TIME: 5 minutes

TOTAL COOKING TIME: 10 minutes

Serving Suggestions & Variations

• Top biscuits and gravy with crumbled vegan sausage or smoked tempeh.

• Go beyond the traditional flavors and add minced fresh thyme, sage, or even rosemary to make it into an herb gravy.

Cheryl's Favorite Citrus Collards

▶ SOY-FREE ▶ GLUTEN-FREE ▶ OIL-FREE

These greens have a great citrus flavor that masks the bitterness of collards that some people shy away from.

1 cup (235 ml) water, plus more as needed

1 teaspoon not-chicken bouillon

5 to 6 cups (about 216 g) collards, washed and tough stems removed

Juice of 2 mandarin oranges or 1 cup (235 ml) orange or tangerine juice

A few dashes liquid smoke

1 tablespoon (15 ml) tangerine balsamic vinegar

Salt, to taste (optional)

In a large skillet, heat the water and bouillon over medium heat. Add the greens in batches so the greens in the pan have cooked down enough to add more. Add more water if needed and cook until tender, about 15 minutes.

Add the juice, liquid smoke, and balsamic vinegar. Taste and adjust the seasoning, if needed. Also add salt, if needed. (If your bouillon has salt, you may not need to add any.)

....

YIELD: 4 servings

PER 1-CUP (54 G) SERVING: 47.5 calories; 0 g total fat; 0 g saturated fat; 1.9 g protein; 7.4 g carbohydrate; 2.2 g dietary fiber; 0 mg cholesterol.

TOTAL PREP TIME: 20 minutes

TOTAL COOKING TIME: 15 minutes

Enchanted Vanilla Pancakes

▶ SOY-FREE OPTION* ▶ GLUTEN-FREE OPTION** ▶ OIL-FREE OPTION***

Pancakes are an easy breakfast treat. These are enchanted with the nutritional power of beans and full of whole grain goodness! Try them with the Chai-Spiced Peach Compote for an over-the-top experience.

FOR THE DRY INGREDIENTS

1 cup (120 g) whole wheat pastry flour (**use gluten-free)

1 teaspoon baking powder

¼ teaspoon salt

FOR THE WET INGREDIENTS

1½ cups (269 g) cooked white beans or 1 can (15 ounces, or 425 g), rinsed and drained

1½ cups (355 ml) unsweetened nondairy milk (vanilla, if possible) (*use soy-free)

½ cup (40 g) rolled oats (**make sure they are marked gluten-free)

2 tablespoons (28 ml) olive oil (***use water)

2 tablespoons (26 g) sugar or (40 g) agave nectar

1 tablespoon (14 g) ground flaxseed mixed with 2 tablespoons (28 ml) warm water

1 teaspoon vanilla extract

::

YIELD: 12 regular-size pancakes or 24 mini pancakes plus 2½ to 3 cups compote (625 to 750 g)

PER REGULAR-SIZE PANCAKE + COMPOTE: 112.3 calories; 3.6 g total fat; 1.0 g saturated fat; 3.3 g protein; 15.5 g carbohydrate; 3.4 g dietary fiber; 0 mg cholesterol.

TOTAL PREP TIME: 20 minutes

TOTAL COOKING TIME: 20 minutes

To prepare the dry ingredients, mix all the ingredients in a large bowl.

To prepare the wet ingredients, add all the ingredients to a food processor and purée. Add the purée to the dry ingredients. Mix with a wooden spoon until thoroughly combined.

Heat a nonstick skillet over medium heat. You can cook a few at a time, but make sure not to crowd them in the pan. Cook until you can see a few bubbles on the top and the edges are dry, then flip and cook a few minutes more until the pancake is cooked through.

Chai-Spiced Peach Compote

5 peaches

1 teaspoon cinnamon

¾ teaspoon cardamom

¼ teaspoon allspice

¼ teaspoon nutmeg

Sweetener of your choice, to taste

To prepare the compote, cut the peaches in half, remove the stone, and remove the peel. If the peaches are ripe enough, the skins will peel off easily. Cut into small pieces.

Add all of the ingredients to a saucepan and bring to a simmer over medium-high heat. Decrease the heat to low, cover, and cook for 15 to 20 minutes until the fruit is cooked through.

Blueberry Almond Oatmeal Pancakes

▶ SOY-FREE OPTION* ▶ GLUTEN-FREE OPTION** ▶ OIL-FREE

These pancakes are gluten-free, easy to make, and they don't require a lot of special ingredients. This is a must-have recipe if you have gluten-free friends coming over for brunch.

FOR THE DRY INGREDIENTS

1 cup (96 g) rolled oats, processed in a food processor to a coarse flour texture (**make sure they are marked gluten-free)

½ cup (56 g) almond meal

¼ cup (40 g) brown rice flour

1 teaspoon baking powder

½ teaspoon baking soda

¼ teaspoon salt

½ teaspoon cardamom

FOR THE WET INGREDIENTS

1½ cups (269 g) cooked white beans or 1 can (15 ounces, or 425 g), rinsed and drained

1½ cups (355 ml) unsweetened nondairy milk (*use soy-free)

2 tablespoons (14 g) ground flaxseed mixed with ¼ cup (60 ml) warm water

1 tablespoon (15 g) sugar

1½ teaspoons vanilla extract

½ teaspoon almond extract

1½ cups (220 g) blueberries, fresh or frozen

To prepare the dry ingredients, mix all the ingredients in a large bowl. Set aside.

To prepare the wet ingredients, add all the ingredients except for the blueberries to a food processor and purée.

Add the purée to the dry ingredients. Mix with a wooden spoon until thoroughly combined. Gently fold in the blueberries.

Heat a nonstick skillet over medium–low heat. Drop the batter by the spoonful onto the pan. You can cook a few at a time, but don't crowd them in the pan. You will want to use a large spatula to flip these because they are not as sturdy as pancakes that contain gluten.

Cook until the entire top surface of the pancake looks dry and then flip and cook a few minutes more until the pancake is cooked through.

:::

YIELD: 10 pancakes

PER PANCAKE: 172.9 calories; 5.5 g total fat; 1.2 g saturated fat; 6.4 g protein; 22.2 g carbohydrate; 5.1 g dietary fiber; 0 mg cholesterol.

TOTAL PREP TIME: 20 minutes

TOTAL COOKING TIME: 20 minutes

Red Bean-Filled Mini Muffins or Baked Donuts

▶ SOY-FREE OPTION* ▶ GLUTEN-FREE OPTION** ▶ OIL-FREE OPTION***

Not only does the batter have red bean paste, but if you make the mini muffins you also add a dollop right in the center. Red bean paste is made from adzuki beans and used in many Asian desserts.

FOR THE DRY INGREDIENTS

¾ cup (90 g) whole wheat pastry flour (**use gluten-free)

¼ teaspoon baking soda

¼ teaspoon baking powder

¼ teaspoon salt

FOR THE WET INGREDIENTS

⅔ cup (160 ml) unsweetened nondairy milk (*use soy-free)

⅔ cup (115 g) Sweet Red Bean Paste (page 27)

¼ teaspoon apple cider vinegar

2 tablespoons (22 g) Sweet Red Bean Paste, for filled muffins

:::

YIELD: 12 mini muffins or mini donuts

PER FILLED MUFFIN: 76.3 calories; 0.7 g total fat; 0.3 g saturated fat; 4.0 g protein; 12.7 g carbohydrate; 1.5 g dietary fiber; 2.2 mg cholesterol.

PER DONUT: 68.9 calories; 0.7 g total fat; 0.3 g saturated fat; 4.0 g protein; 11.6 g carbohydrate; 1.4 g dietary fiber; 2.2 mg cholesterol.

TOTAL PREP TIME: 10 minutes

TOTAL COOKING TIME: 10 to 15 minutes

Preheat the oven to 350°F (180°C, or gas mark 4). Oil a mini muffin pan or mini donut pan ***or line with paper liners.

To prepare the dry ingredients, mix all the ingredients in a large bowl. Set aside.

To prepare the wet ingredients, add all the ingredients to a small bowl and mix with a whisk to help break up the bean paste. Add the wet ingredients to the dry ingredients and mix with a wooden spoon.

For the filled muffins: Spread about 2 teaspoons of the mixture in each muffin cup to cover the bottom. Then add ½ teaspoon of extra red bean paste in the center. Top with about 1 tablespoon (15 g) of the batter and press a little so it covers the sides and none of the red bean paste in the middle shows. Bake for 12 to 15 minutes.

For the donuts: Scoop the mixture into a mini-donut pan. I use a small cookie scoop, which gives you just the right amount. Then turn the scoop over and pat the middle so the post shows through the center. This ensures you'll get a good hole in your donut. Bake for 10 minutes.

Orange Blossom Brunch Biscuits

▶ SOY-FREE OPTION* ▶ GLUTEN-FREE OPTION** ▶ OIL-FREE OPTION***

These remind me of those taboo out-of-a-can biscuits with their bright taste of orange included in the batter and glaze to up the flavor. You can feel good about these, though, because they are made with whole wheat and amped up with bean protein and fiber!

FOR THE DRY INGREDIENTS

2 cups (240 g) whole wheat pastry flour (**use gluten-free)

2 teaspoons baking powder

1 teaspoon baking soda

¼ teaspoon salt

FOR THE WET INGREDIENTS

1½ cups (269 g) cooked white beans or 1 can (15 ounces, or 425 g), rinsed and drained

¼ cup (60 ml) orange juice

¼ cup (60 ml) unsweetened nondairy milk (plain or vanilla) (*use soy-free)

2 tablespoons (28 ml) olive oil (***use water)

2 tablespoons (40 g) agave nectar

1 tablespoon (6 g) orange zest

1 teaspoon vanilla extract

FOR THE GLAZE

⅓ cup (42 g) powdered sugar

1 tablespoon (6 g) orange zest

1 to 2 tablespoons (14 to 28 ml) orange juice or nondairy milk

::

YIELD: 12 biscuits

PER BISCUIT: 145.2 calories; 2.8 g total fat; 0.4 g saturated fat; 3.6 g protein; 27.1 g carbohydrate; 4.2 g dietary fiber; 0 mg cholesterol.

TOTAL PREP TIME: 25 minutes

TOTAL COOKING TIME: 15 to 20 minutes

Preheat the oven to 350°F (180°C, or gas mark 4) and oil a baking sheet ***or line with parchment paper.

To prepare the dry ingredients, mix all the ingredients in a large bowl. Set aside.

To prepare the wet ingredients, add all the ingredients to a food processor and purée. Add the purée to the dry ingredients. (If it's too dry, add 1 tablespoon [15 ml] nondairy milk.) Mix with a wooden spoon and turn out onto a floured cutting board.

Lightly knead until completely mixed, adding a little more flour as needed. Pat the dough out to about a 1-inch (2.5 cm) thickness. Using a round cookie cutter or drinking glass, cut out biscuits and place on the prepared baking sheet. Gather the leftover dough into a ball, flour the cutting board, pat down to about 1 inch (2.5 cm) thick again, and cut more biscuits. Repeat until you don't have enough dough to make a same sized biscuit. You should end up with 12 biscuits. Bake for 15 to 20 minutes.

To make the glaze, mix the glaze ingredients together in a small bowl. This allows for about ½ teaspoon glaze per biscuit. Spread the glaze on the biscuits and serve warm or at room temperature.

3

NOSHY BEANS

Appetizers, Dips, and Spreads

Beans make the best spreads and dips. They make a great stuffing for celery or endive, not to mention how tasty they are on bruschetta or as a pizza base. (Just make them bite-size for your cocktail parties and more meal-size for TV night in with your friends.)

Four-Layer Bean Dip

▶ GLUTEN-FREE ▶ OIL-FREE ▶ SOY-FREE OPTION*

Sometimes you need a quick and dirty dip for a party. This is simple to make, but dressed up with a little rum in the beans and some chile in the vegan sour cream and then topped with multicolored heirloom tomatoes.

1 can (15 ounces, or 425 g) refried black beans or 1½ cups (357 g) homemade

Zest and juice of 1 lime

2 teaspoons rum

¼ to ½ teaspoon chipotle powder

¼ cup (60 g) vegan sour cream *or Cashew Cream (page 28)

2 tablespoons (18 g) chopped green chiles

1 avocado, peeled, pitted, and mashed

¼ cup (65 g) salsa verde

1 to 2 cups (180 to 360 g) chopped heirloom tomatoes

Smoked salt, to taste

:::

YIELD: 3 cups (920 g)

PER ½-CUP (155 G) SERVING: 149.8 calories; 6.7 g total fat; 1.4 g saturated fat; 4.8 g protein; 17.0 g carbohydrate; 6.6 g dietary fiber; 0 mg cholesterol.

TOTAL PREP TIME: 15 minutes

LAYER 1: BEANS
Add the beans, lime zest and juice, rum, and chipotle powder to a food processor and process until smooth. You may need to scrape down and process a bit more. Spread on the bottom of your serving plate.

LAYER 2: SOUR CREAM
Combine the sour cream and chilies in a small bowl. Spread over the beans but leave a bit of the beans showing.

LAYER 3: GREEN GUAC
Mix together the mashed avocado and the salsa verde. Spread over the sour cream.

LAYER 4: MULTICOLORED HEIRLOOM TOMATOES
Sprinkle the tomatoes with the smoked salt and layer over the top.

Fancy Bean Substitutes: Black Calypso, Vaquero, Purple Runner

Creamy Spinach Artichoke White Bean Dip

▶ SOY-FREE ▶ GLUTEN-FREE ▶ OIL-FREE OPTION*

This is the healthiest spinach artichoke dip I've ever made. There is oil involved in the base recipe, but it can easily be left out to accommodate a no-oil-added diet.

1½ cups (269 g) cooked white beans or 1 can (15 ounces, or 425 g), rinsed and drained

½ cup (120 ml) unsweetened coconut milk

⅓ cup (32 g) nutritional yeast

1 tablespoon (15 ml) olive oil (*omit)

¼ teaspoon liquid smoke

1 to 2 tablespoons (15 to 28 ml) olive oil (*use water)

½ small onion, minced

2 cloves garlic, minced

1 bag (16 ounces, or 455 g) frozen chopped spinach (or the same amount fresh)

1 can (8.5 ounces, or 240 g) artichoke hearts, chopped

¾ teaspoon nutmeg

Salt and pepper, to taste

:::

YIELD: 4 cups (1150 g)

PER ½-CUP (145 G) SERVING: 90.1 calories; 2.2 g total fat; 0.6 g saturated fat; 5.0 g protein; 12.3 g carbohydrate; 4.0 g dietary fiber; 0 mg cholesterol.

TOTAL PREP TIME: 15 minutes

TOTAL COOKING TIME: 20 minutes

Combine the beans, coconut milk, nutritional yeast, olive oil (if using), and liquid smoke in a food processor. Process until smooth. Set aside.

Heat the olive oil (or water) in a sauté pan over medium heat, add the onion, and cook until translucent, about 5 minutes. Add the garlic and sauté for 1 minute more.

Add the frozen spinach and chopped artichoke hearts and cook until warmed through, about 15 minutes. Add the bean mixture, stir to combine, and then add the nutmeg and salt and pepper to taste.

Serving Suggestions & Variations

Serve with toasted bread, with corn chips, or even in mini grilled sandwiches.

Fancy Bean Substitutes: Flageolet, European Solider, Vallarta, Alubia Blanca

White Bean Pecan Paté

▶ SOY-FREE ▶ GLUTEN-FREE ▶ OIL-FREE

This is a super quick and easy appetizer to throw together for an impromptu cocktail party. It's not the prettiest dip on the block, but it just might be the tastiest!

1½ cups (269 g) cooked white beans or 1 can (15 ounces, or 425 g), rinsed and drained

¼ to ½ cup (60 to 120 ml) water

½ cup (55 g) pecans

⅓ cup (32 g) nutritional yeast

½ teaspoon basil

½ teaspoon oregano

¼ teaspoon granulated garlic or 1 small clove garlic, minced

¼ to ½ teaspoon smoked salt

YIELD: 3 cups (450 g)

PER ½-CUP (75 G) SERVING: 142.4 calories; 7.4 g total fat; 0.6 g saturated fat; 6.1 g protein; 14.4 g carbohydrate; 5.4 g dietary fiber; 0 mg cholesterol.

TOTAL PREP TIME: 10 minutes

Add everything except for the smoked salt to the food processor and blend until smooth. Taste, add salt, blend, and taste again. Add more salt if necessary.

Serving Suggestions & Variations

To make white bean arugula pesto, add a handful of arugula to the food processor and purée. Add a little water if you need to thin the mixture so it can process smoothly. Taste and add more arugula little by little until it's just the way you like it.

This pesto goes great over pasta. Just cook pasta and reserve about 1 cup (235 ml) of the pasta water. Add the water ¼ cup (60 ml) by ¼ cup (60 ml) into the pesto until it's just thin enough to coat the pasta.

Fancy Bean Substitutes: Flageolet, European Solider, Vallarta, Alubia Blanca

Almond Cheez Spread (Faux Goat Cheese)

▶ SOY-FREE OPTION* ▶ GLUTEN-FREE
▶ OIL-FREE

I miss the the tart flavor of goat cheese. This almond spread is the perfect substitute.

1½ cups (269 g) cooked white beans or 1 can (15 ounces, or 425 g), rinsed and drained

1 cup (110 g) skinned slivered almonds

½ cup (120 ml) unsweetened nondairy milk (*use soy-free)

¼ cup (34 g) macadamia nuts

Juice of 1 lemon

1 tablespoon (6 g) nutritional yeast

2 teaspoons apple cider vinegar

1 teaspoon salt

Black pepper, to taste

Add all the ingredients to a food processor and process until smooth. This will take a few minutes, so stop occasionally and scrape down the sides of the bowl, then process some more. Add water, 1 tablespoon (15 ml) at a time, if it's too thick for your food processor or taste.

Serve with crackers, on salads, or cooked in other dishes.

YIELD: 3 cups (750 g)

PER ¼-CUP (63 G) SERVING: 83.5 calories; 4.7 g total fat; 0.8 g saturated fat; 3.4 g protein; 7.6 g carbohydrate; 2.4 g dietary fiber; 0.2 mg cholesterol.

TOTAL PREP TIME: 10 minutes

Fancy Bean Substitutes: Flageolet, European Solider, Vallarta, Alubia Blanca

White Bean Basil Cheezy Spread

▶ SOY-FREE ▶ GLUTEN-FREE ▶ OIL-FREE

This is my favorite pizza base and is wonderful topped with some crumbled veggie sausage and chopped black olives. (It's nut-free, too!)

1½ cups (269 g) cooked white beans or 1 can (15 ounces, or 425 g), rinsed and drained

¼ cup (24 g) nutritional yeast

1 teaspoon lemon juice

½ teaspoon lemon zest

½ teaspoon granulated garlic or 1 clove garlic, minced

Salt and pepper, to taste

2 tablespoons (5 g) chopped fresh basil

Place everything except the salt, pepper, and fresh basil into a food processor and blend until smooth, scraping down the sides of the container as needed. Season with salt and pepper and then blend again.

Put the mixture in a bowl and mix the basil in by hand. You can do it in the food processor, but it will have a green tint to it instead of green flecks.

YIELD: 2 cups (500 g)

PER ¼-CUP (63 G) SERVING: 40.1 calories; 0.1 g total fat; 0 g saturated fat; 3.0 g protein; 7.9 g carbohydrate; 2.7 g dietary fiber; 0 mg cholesterol.

TOTAL PREP TIME: 10 minutes

Fancy Bean Substitutes: Flageolet, European Solider, Vallarta, Alubia Blanca

Smoky White Bean Spread

▶ SOY-FREE ▶ GLUTEN-FREE ▶ OIL-FREE

This thick and rich spread is perfect for a light meal, cocktail party, or on top of a veggie burger.

3 cups (537 g) cooked white beans or 2 cans (15 ounces, or 425 g each), rinsed and drained

½ cup (70 g) raw cashews

1 teaspoon smoked paprika

½ to 1 teaspoon liquid smoke

½ to 1 teaspoon smoked salt

½ teaspoon apple cider vinegar or white vinegar

¼ teaspoon mustard powder

½ cup (120 ml) water (optional)

½ cup (48 g) nutritional yeast

Add all the ingredients except for the optional water and nutritional yeast to a food processor or blender. Blend until smooth, which may take as long as 5 minutes. Stop and scrape down the sides if needed.

If the mixture is too thick for your taste or your blender, add the water and blend.

Once smooth, add the nutritional yeast and blend one more time.

YIELD: 4½ cups (1125 g)

PER ½-CUP (125 G) SERVING: 249.0 calories; 7.3 g total fat; 0 g saturated fat; 14.6 g protein; 35.3 g carbohydrate; 10.7 g dietary fiber; 0 mg cholesterol.

TOTAL PREP TIME: 10 minutes

Fancy Bean Substitutes: Flageolet, European Solider, Vallarta, Alubia Blanca

Pepita Black Bean Dip ▶

▶ SOY-FREE ▶ GLUTEN-FREE ▶ OIL-FREE

The puréed pumpkin seeds give this dip an earthy flavor. If you like yours spicier, add chipotle and a little adobo sauce to jazz it up and make it more fiery.

1½ cups (269 g) cooked black beans or 1 can (15 ounces, or 425 g), rinsed and drained

½ cup (114 g) roasted, salted pepitas

¼ cup (60 ml) water

Juice of 1 lime

2 tablespoons (18 g) chopped green chiles

¼ teaspoon ground cumin

¼ teaspoon lime zest, plus more for garnish (optional)

⅛ to ¼ teaspoon cayenne or other spicy pepper

1 chipotle in adobo sauce (optional)

Salt (optional)

Blend everything together (except for the salt) until smooth in a food processor or blender. Taste, season with salt if desired, and blend again. Garnish with extra lime zest, if desired.

Serve chilled with tortilla chips or hot in burritos or tacos.

YIELD: 2 cups (500 g)

PER ½-CUP (125 G) SERVING: 148.2 calories; 4.4 g total fat; 0.8 g saturated fat; 8.7 g protein; 17.9 g carbohydrate; 5.2 g dietary fiber; 0 mg cholesterol.

TOTAL PREP TIME: 15 minutes

Fancy Bean Substitutes: Black Calypso, Vaquero, Purple Runner

Vegan Cashew-Bean Queso

▶ SOY-FREE OPTION* ▶ GLUTEN-FREE ▶ OIL-FREE

Here's a soy-free and oil-free queso substitution that even looks like the real thing. People go crazy for this dip!

1½ cups (269 g) cooked white beans or 1 can (15 ounces, or 425 g), rinsed and drained

½ cup (70 g) raw cashews

¼ cup (24 g) nutritional yeast

½ cup (120 ml) nondairy milk (unsweetened is best) (*use soy-free)

1 to 2 tablespoons (9 to 18 g) chopped green chiles

1 teaspoon chili powder

1 teaspoon smoked paprika

½ to 1 teaspoon salt

A few slices pickled or fresh jalapeño (optional)

::::::::::::::::::::::::::::::::::::::

YIELD: 3 cups (600 g)

PER ½-CUP (100 G) SERVING: 88.6 calories; 3.9 g total fat; 0.3 g saturated fat; 4.4 g protein; 10.0 g carbohydrate; 2.7 g dietary fiber; 0 mg cholesterol.

TOTAL PREP TIME: 15 minutes

Add everything to a food processor or blender and process until smooth. Taste and adjust the seasonings as needed. Feel free to add hot chili powder for more heat. You can warm this on the stove top, in the microwave, or in a slow cooker, if desired.

Serving Suggestions & Variations

If you'd prefer a thinner sauce, add an extra ½ cup (120 ml) nondairy milk.

Fancy Bean Substitutes: Flageolet, European Solider, Vallarta, Alubia Blanca

Black-Eyed Pea Corn Bites

▶ SOY-FREE OPTION* ▶ GLUTEN-FREE OPTION** ▶ OIL-FREE OPTION***

These are a great last-minute cocktail party treat, and you can whip them up with ingredients already in your pantry.

FOR THE DRY INGREDIENTS

1 cup (120 g) whole wheat pastry flour (**use gluten-free)

1 cup (140 g) cornmeal

1 teaspoon baking powder

½ teaspoon baking soda

½ teaspoon ground cumin

½ teaspoon chipotle powder

¼ teaspoon salt

FOR THE WET INGREDIENTS

2 cups (475 ml) unsweetened coconut milk or other nondairy milk (*use soy-free)

1½ cups (246 g) corn kernels

1½ cups (248 g) cooked black-eyed peas or 1 can (15 ounces, or 425 g), rinsed and drained

Preheat the oven to 350°F (180°C, or gas mark 4). Oil three (12-muffin) mini muffin pans ***or line with paper liners.

To prepare the dry ingredients, mix all the ingredients together in a large bowl.

To prepare the wet ingredients, add the wet ingredients to the dry and mix until combined. Fill the muffin tins with the mixture and bake 12 to 15 minutes.

Fancy Bean Substitutes: Yellow-Eyed Peas, Rio Zape, Vaquero Beans

:::

YIELD: 36 mini muffins

PER MINI MUFFIN: 40.2 calories; 0.6 g total fat; 0.3 g saturated fat; 1.3 g protein; 7.8 g carbohydrate; 1.5 g dietary fiber; 0 mg cholesterol.

TOTAL PREP TIME: 15 minutes

TOTAL COOKING TIME: 12 to 15 minutes

Beany Eggplant Bruschetta Spread

▶ SOY-FREE ▶ GLUTEN-FREE ▶ OIL-FREE OPTION*

A thick, savory dip that makes a crazy-good bruschetta, this recipe has a delicious rich flavor from the sun-dried tomatoes and a fresh taste from the basil.

1 to 2 tablespoons (15 to 28 ml) olive oil (*use water)

½ small onion, minced

3 cloves garlic, minced

2 cups (164 g) chopped eggplant

1 cup (235 ml) water

2 tablespoons (7 g) chopped sun-dried tomatoes

½ teaspoon oregano

1½ cups (269 g) cooked white beans or 1 can (15 ounces, or 425 g), rinsed and drained

⅓ cup (13 g) fresh basil, chopped

Salt and pepper, to taste

Heat the oil in a large sauté pan over medium heat and cook the onion until translucent, about 5 minutes. Add the garlic and sauté 1 minute more.

Add the eggplant, water, sun-dried tomatoes, and oregano and cook until the eggplant is translucent and soft, 15 to 20 minutes.

Combine the eggplant mixture with the beans and basil in a food processor and process until smooth. Add salt and pepper to taste.

Fancy Bean Substitutes: Flageolet, European Solider, Vallarta, Alubia Blanca

YIELD: 4 cups (720 g)

PER ½-CUP (90 G) SERVING: 100.6 calories; 5.0 g total fat; 0.6 g saturated fat; 3.6 g protein; 10.9 g carbohydrate; 2.5 g dietary fiber; 0 mg cholesterol.

TOTAL PREP TIME: 20 minutes

TOTAL COOKING TIME: 20 to 25 minutes

4

NUTRITIOUS SOUPS

Easy and Delicious One-Bowl Meals

Soups are hearty one-bowl meals and a great way to use up whatever veggies you have in the fridge. I keep a few servings of soup in the freezer at all times. That keeps me eating healthy no matter how tired I might be.

Get-Well-Fast Chickpea and Rice Soup

▶ SOY-FREE ▶ GLUTEN-FREE ▶ OIL-FREE

This is a soup I like to always have in the freezer. It's just what I need if I've caught a cold or just feel a little off.

3 cups (492 g) cooked chickpeas or 2 cans (15 ounces, or 425 g each), rinsed and drained

7 cloves garlic, minced

2 cups (260 g) diced carrots (peeled if not organic)

1 cup (100 g) diced celery

¼ cup (24 g) veggie bouillon

2 bay leaves

3 sprigs fresh thyme or 1 teaspoon dried

1 sprig fresh rosemary or ½ teaspoon ground

10 cups (2.4 L) water

1 cup (185 g) brown rice

½ cup (48 g) nutritional yeast

Salt and pepper, to taste

::

YIELD: 6 servings

PER 1½-CUP (355 ML) SERVING: 272.5 calories; 3.0 g total fat; 0.2 g saturated fat; 11.9 g protein; 34.3 g carbohydrate; 8.3 g dietary fiber; 0 mg cholesterol.

TOTAL PREP TIME: 15 minutes

TOTAL COOKING TIME: 60 minutes to 75 minutes for stove top, 6 to 8 hours for slow cooker

STOVE-TOP DIRECTIONS

Add everything except the nutritional yeast, salt, and pepper to a large stockpot. Bring to a boil and then decrease the heat to low. Cook until the rice is done, about 45 to 60 minutes.

Stir in the nutritional yeast, salt, and pepper and then taste. Adjust the other seasonings as needed. Remove the bay leaves and herb sprigs. Serve and freeze the leftovers for a sniffly day. You can add some extra fresh garlic to the soup you're freezing to give yourself a get-well boost. It will mellow some when you heat it a second time.

SLOW COOKER DIRECTIONS

Use 8 cups (1.9 L) water and 3 cups (585 g) cooked brown rice instead of raw rice. (You can use raw rice, but it will break down significantly if it cooks overnight, so it will be a muddier soup. If you choose to use raw rice, you may have to adjust the water up as well.)

Add everything except the cooked brown rice, nutritional yeast, salt, and pepper to a 6-quart (5.7 L) slow cooker. Cook for 6 to 8 hours on low. Add the cooked brown rice, nutritional yeast, and salt and pepper to taste. Add extra fresh garlic if needed.

Fancy Bean Substitutes: Scarlet Runner Beans, Tepary, Good Mother Stallard

Hutterite Soup

▶ SOY-FREE ▶ GLUTEN-FREE ▶ OIL-FREE

Hutterite beans are another heirloom bean that you can use in place of pinto beans. And of course, pinto beans work beautifully in this soup as well.

3 cups (513 g) cooked Hutterite beans or 2 cans (15 ounces, or 425 g each) pinto beans, rinsed and drained

3 cloves garlic, minced

2 carrots, diced (peeled if not organic)

2 stalks celery, diced

2 cups (180 g) finely chopped cabbage

2 cups (300 g) diced turnip, (220 g) potato, or (300 g) rutabaga, or a mix

4 cups (950 ml) water

3 veggie bouillon cubes

1 teaspoon oregano

1 teaspoon smoked paprika

1 teaspoon ground cumin

½ teaspoon ground jalapeño or 1 fresh, seeded and minced

Salt and pepper, to taste

::

YIELD: 6 servings

PER 1½-CUP (355 ML) SERVING: 136.5 calories; 0.7 g total fat; 0 g saturated fat; 7.1 g protein; 30.2 g carbohydrate; 10.0 g dietary fiber; 0 mg cholesterol.

TOTAL PREP TIME: 20 minutes

TOTAL COOKING TIME: 45 minutes for stove top, 6 to 9 hours for slow cooker

STOVE-TOP DIRECTIONS

Add everything except the salt and pepper to a large soup pot. Cook over medium-low heat until the root veggies are tender and can easily be pierced with a fork, about 45 minutes. All the flavors will meld. Add salt and pepper and adjust the other seasonings as needed.

SLOW COOKER DIRECTIONS

Add everything except the salt and pepper to the slow cooker. Cook on low for 6 to 9 hours. Taste and add salt and pepper and adjust other seasonings as needed.

Fancy Bean Substitutes: Rio Zape, Goat's Eye, Cranberry

New Year's Soup with Black-Eyed Peas

▶ SOY-FREE ▶ GLUTEN-FREE ▶ OIL-FREE OPTION*

It's ingrained in Southerners that on New Year's Day there are a few things you must eat to start the year off right. Greens, traditionally collards, are said to bring more money into your life, and black-eyed peas bring good luck. For this recipe, you can get fancy and use yellow-eyed peas instead. Either way, this soup will still make your New Year's Day lunch one of the highlights of your year. That's my idea of good luck!

2 tablespoons (28 ml) olive oil (*use water or broth)

½ small onion, minced

2 cloves garlic, minced

½ green or red bell pepper, cored, seeded, and minced

4½ cups (743 g) cooked black-eyed peas or 3 cans (15 ounces, or 425 g each), rinsed and drained

1 medium sweet potato, peeled and chopped small

½ cup (93 g) long-grain brown rice

5 cups (1.2 L) water

1 tablespoon (6 g) bouillon or 1 cube

½ teaspoon salt

⅛ to ¼ teaspoon liquid smoke

Black pepper, to taste

::

YIELD: 6 servings

PER 1½-CUP (355 ML) SERVING: 208.8 calories; 5.2 g total fat; 0.8 g saturated fat; 7.1 g protein; 32.4 g carbohydrate; 6.7 g dietary fiber; 0 mg cholesterol.

TOTAL PREP TIME: 20 minutes

TOTAL COOKING TIME: 35 to 65 minutes for stove top, 7 to 9 hours for slow cooker

STOVE-TOP DIRECTIONS

Heat the oil in a 2-quart (1.8 L) sauté pan over medium heat. Add the onion and sauté until translucent, about 5 minutes. Add the garlic and bell pepper and sauté for 2 minutes more.

Add the peas, sweet potato, rice, water, bouillon, salt, and liquid smoke and stir to combine. Cook over medium heat, uncovered, for 30 to 60 minutes, or until the potatoes are easily pierced with a fork. Season with pepper.

SLOW COOKER DIRECTIONS

Heat the oil in a 2-quart (1.8 L) sauté pan over medium heat. Add the onion and sauté until translucent, about 5 minutes. Add the garlic and bell pepper and sauté for 2 minutes more.

Add the sautéed veggies, sweet potato, rice, water, bouillon, salt, and liquid smoke to a 4- or 5-quart (3.8 or 4.7 L) slow cooker. Cook on low for 7 to 9 hours. The rice will break down and thicken the soup in the slow cooker. Add pepper to taste. Taste and add more salt or liquid smoke if needed.

Serving Suggestions & Variations

Go ahead and complete your New Year's meal by adding about 2 cups (72 g) chopped collard greens to the soup in the last 10 to 15 minutes of cooking.

Fancy Bean Substitutes: Yellow-Eyed Peas, Cranberry

Moroccan Chickpea Soup

▶ SOY-FREE ▶ OIL-FREE OPTION* ▶ GLUTEN-FREE OPTION**

Sometimes you need a soup full of flavor that's easy to make after a hard day, and this is one you will turn to again and again.

1 tablespoon (28 ml) olive oil (*use water or broth)

1 small onion, minced

2 cloves garlic, minced

½ green bell pepper, minced

3 small carrots, minced (peeled if not organic)

1½ teaspoons ground cumin

1½ teaspoons paprika

1 teaspoon cinnamon

½ teaspoon each ground ginger, ground coriander, and allspice

⅛ to ¼ teaspoon cayenne pepper

1 can (14.5 ounces, or 410 g) diced tomatoes or 1½ cups (270 g) chopped fresh

3 cups (492 g) cooked chickpeas or 2 cans (15 ounces, or 425 g each), rinsed and drained

4 cups (950 ml) water

Pinch of saffron

Salt and pepper, to taste

1½ cups (236 g) cooked whole wheat couscous, **or (278 g) quinoa, or (174 g) millet, for serving

Chopped fresh mint or parsley, for serving

Lemon wedges, for serving

STOVE-TOP DIRECTIONS

Heat the olive oil in a large saucepan over medium heat. Add the onion and sauté until translucent, about 5 minutes.

Add the garlic, bell pepper, carrot, and all the spices. Decrease the heat to low and sauté for about 1 minute until the spices become more fragrant.

Add the tomatoes, chickpeas, 4 cups (950 ml) water, and saffron and increase the heat to medium. Cook, covered, until the carrots are tender, 20 to 30 minutes.

Taste and add salt and pepper. Now is also the time to adjust the spices if you'd like it hotter.

Spoon the cooked couscous into bowls and top with the mixture. Serve with the fresh herbs and lemon wedges so people can adjust the flavors as desired.

SLOW COOKER DIRECTIONS

Heat the oil in a sauté pan over medium heat, add the onion and sauté until translucent, and then add the garlic and cook 1 minute more.

Add the cooked mixture to a slow cooker with the green pepper, carrot, spices, tomatoes, 2½ cups (about 570 ml) water (note—less than the stove top recipe) and saffron. Cook on low 8 to 10 hours. Add salt and pepper to taste, and adjust spices as needed.

::

YIELD: 6 servings

PER 1½-CUP (355 ML) SERVING: 188.6 calories; 4.9 g total fat; 0.6 g saturated fat; 8.6 g protein; 31.2 g carbohydrate; 8.3 g dietary fiber; 0 mg cholesterol.

TOTAL PREP TIME: 20 minutes

TOTAL COOKING TIME: 40 minutes for stove top, 8 to 10 hours for slow cooker

Fancy Bean Substitutes: Scarlet Runner Beans, Tepary, Good Mother Stallard

Indian Split Pea and Mung Bean Soup

▶ SOY-FREE ▶ GLUTEN-FREE ▶ OIL-FREE OPTION*

This soup uses whole mung beans, which you may already have around to make your own bean sprouts. Add in some split peas and wonderful Indian spices and you have a really unique pea soup.

2 tablespoons (28 ml) olive oil (*use water or broth)

½ small onion, minced

2 cloves garlic, minced

1 teaspoon fenugreek seeds

2 teaspoons mustard seeds

1 teaspoon turmeric

½ teaspoon ground cumin

½ cup (104 g) whole mung beans

5 cups (1.2 L) water, divided

½ cup (113 g) green split peas

1 tablespoon (8 g) grated ginger root

2 carrots, diced (peeled if not organic)

½ teaspoon ground coriander

¼ teaspoon red pepper flakes or chili powder (optional)

Salt, to taste

:::

YIELD: 4 servings

PER 1½-CUP (355 ML) SERVING: 230.8 calories; 10.9 g total fat; 1.2 g saturated fat; 11.3 g protein; 28.3 g carbohydrate; 4.7 g dietary fiber; 0 mg cholesterol.

TOTAL PREP TIME: 20 minutes

TOTAL COOKING TIME: 70 minutes

In a soup pot, heat the oil over medium heat, add the onion, and cook until translucent, about 5 minutes. Add the garlic, fenugreek seeds, mustard seeds, turmeric, and cumin. Sauté for about 2 minutes until the spices start releasing their oils (they'll start smelling stronger).

Add the mung beans and 4 cups (950 ml) of the water and increase the heat to high. Once it just starts to boil, decrease the heat to low, cover, and cook for 30 minutes.

Add the split peas, ginger, carrots, coriander, and red pepper flakes and stir to combine. Add the remaining 1 cup (235 ml) water if it's getting too thick. Cook for 30 more minutes or until the split peas start to melt into the soup and the carrots are tender. Season with salt.

Fancy Bean Substitutes: Red or golden lentils for the split peas, and crowder peas or pigeon peas for the mung beans

Thai Coconut Tongue of Fire Soup

▶ SOY-FREE ▶ GLUTEN-FREE ▶ OIL-FREE

The tongue of fire in the title refers to a variety of heirloom beans with that name, which have a meaty mouthfeel and an undertone of spice in them. They are firm like kidney beans, which you can use in their place if you can't find the exotic ones.

2 cups (475 ml) water

1 can (14 ounces, or 410 ml) light coconut milk

3 cloves garlic, minced

1 tablespoon (15 g) lemongrass paste or 3 pieces lemongrass, smashed with the flat side of a knife (or substitute 1 teaspoon other lemony herbs such as verbena or lemon balm, or 1 teaspoon lemon zest)

1 teaspoon galangal root paste or grated ginger

1 teaspoon kaffir lime leaves (optional)

Two 1-inch-long (2.5 cm) slices ginger

12 fresh shiitake mushrooms, sliced or minced

1½ cups (266 g) cooked Tongue of Fire or kidney beans or 1 can (15 ounces, or 425 g), rinsed and drained

1 cup (164 g) corn kernels

½ teaspoon salt

½ red bell pepper, cored, seeded, and diced

Zest of ½ lime

¼ to ½ teaspoon cayenne pepper

2 tablespoons (2 g) minced cilantro, plus more for serving

Lime wedges, for serving

Put the water, coconut milk, garlic, lemon grass paste, galangal root paste, kaffir lime leaves, ginger, mushrooms, beans, corn, and salt into a large saucepan or small stockpot. Cook uncovered over medium heat for 15 minutes so the flavors can infuse into the broth.

Add the red pepper, lime zest, and cayenne and cook until the veggies are tender but still firm, about 15 more minutes. Add the cilantro and taste and adjust the seasonings if needed.

Serve with the lime wedges and extra cilantro.

Serving Suggestions & Variations

I've found jarred galangal, kaffir lime leaves, and lemon grass in my local grocery, so if you live in or near a city, you may be able to find these exotic ingredients there. If they aren't in a nearby store, you can also get them online. If you can't find the kaffir lime leaves, they can be left out.

Fancy Bean Substitutes: Scarlet Runner Beans, Sangre de Toro

YIELD: 4 servings

PER 1½-CUP (355 ML) SERVING: 187.8 calories; 5.0 g total fat; 3.8 g saturated fat; 6.7 g protein; 28.2 g carbohydrate; 6.9 g dietary fiber; 0 mg cholesterol.

TOTAL PREP TIME: 20 minutes

TOTAL COOKING TIME: 30 minutes

Beluga Lentil Borscht

▶ SOY-FREE OPTION* ▶ GLUTEN-FREE ▶ OIL-FREE OPTION**

There's nothing better on a cold winter's night than a steaming bowl of beet, potato, and cabbage soup. Adding in beluga lentils makes it even heartier. Enjoy with a hunk of homemade bread.

1 tablespoon (28 ml) olive oil (**use water or broth)

1 small onion, minced

3 cloves garlic, minced

1 teaspoon caraway seeds

1 cup (192 g) beluga lentils or regular brown lentils

1 large potato, chopped (peeled if not organic)

2 small carrots, chopped (peeled if not organic)

3 medium beets, peeled and chopped

6 cups (1.4 L) water if cooking on stove top or 4 cups (950 ml) water if cooking in slow cooker

2 bay leaves

3 tablespoons (18 g) veggie bouillon

1 can (14.5 ounces, or 410 g) diced tomatoes or 1½ cups (270 g) chopped fresh

2 teaspoons dried dill weed

1 tablespoon (28 ml) apple cider vinegar

Salt and pepper, to taste

Vegan sour cream or *Cashew Cream (page 28), for serving

::

YIELD: 8 servings

PER 1½-CUP (355 ML) SERVING: 156.3 calories; 2.1 g total fat; 0.3 g saturated fat; 3.1 g protein; 16.7 g carbohydrate; 2.9 g dietary fiber; 0 mg cholesterol.

TOTAL PREP TIME: 20 minutes

TOTAL COOKING TIME: 50 minutes for stove top, 8½ to 10½ hours for slow cooker

STOVE-TOP DIRECTIONS

Heat the olive oil in a large stockpot over medium heat. Add the onion and sauté until translucent, about 5 minutes. Add the garlic and caraway seeds and sauté for 1 minute more.

Add the lentils, potato, carrots, beets, 6 cups (1.4 L) water, bay leaves, and bouillon and stir to combine. Cook until the lentils and beets are tender, about 30 minutes.

Once the lentils are tender, add the tomatoes and dill and cook for 15 more minutes. Just before serving, add the apple cider vinegar, salt, and pepper. Adjust the other herbs and spices as needed. Remove the bay leaves. Serve topped with vegan sour cream, if desired.

SLOW COOKER DIRECTIONS

Heat the oil in a sauté pan over medium heat. Add the onion and sauté until translucent, about 5 minutes. Add the garlic and caraway seeds and sauté for 1 minute more.

Add the cooked mixture to a slow cooker along with the lentils, potato, carrots, beets, 4 cups (950 ml) water, bay leaves, and bouillon and cook on low for 8 to 10 hours.

Once the lentils are tender, add the tomatoes and dill and cook for 30 more minutes on high. Just before serving, add the apple cider vinegar, salt, and pepper. Adjust the other herbs and spices as needed. Remove the bay leaves. Serve topped with vegan sour cream, if desired.

Heartier Cream of Tomato Soup with White Beans

▶ SOY-FREE OPTION* ▶ GLUTEN-FREE ▶ OIL-FREE OPTION**

Adding beans to the traditional tomato soup gives it a lot of body and an infusion of protein. If you have to hide beans from your children, this is the place to start. Make them a grilled vegan cheese sandwich to dip into their soup and they won't even suspect what's in it.

2 tablespoons (28 ml) olive oil (**use water or broth)

½ small onion, minced

3 cloves garlic, minced

1 teaspoon marjoram

1 teaspoon thyme

½ teaspoon smoked paprika

¼ teaspoon ground rosemary

2 cups (475 ml) unsweetened nondairy milk (*use soy-free)

2 cans (14.5 ounces, or 410 g) diced tomatoes or 3 cups (540 g) chopped fresh

1½ cups (269 g) cooked white beans or 1 can (15 ounces, or 425 g), rinsed and drained

Salt and pepper, to taste

Heat the oil over medium heat in a large saucepan, then add the onion and cook until soft and translucent, 5 to 7 minutes. Add the garlic and herbs and then cook for 2 to 3 minutes more.

Add the cooked onion mixture, nondairy milk, tomatoes, and beans to a blender and blend until smooth. (Or you can put everything into the saucepan and use an immersion blender.)

Taste and add salt and pepper to your liking, then pour back into the pot and heat thoroughly for about 15 to 20 minutes over medium-low heat.

It is not quite as smooth as regular tomato soup. To get a silkier consistency, you can either blend it in a high-speed blender or strain it through a mesh strainer.

::

YIELD: 4 servings

PER 1½-CUP (355 ML) SERVING: 199.7 calories; 9.6 g total fat; 3.5 g saturated fat; 6.9 g protein; 26.0 g carbohydrate; 6.5 g dietary fiber; 0 mg cholesterol.

TOTAL PREP TIME: 15 minutes

TOTAL COOKING TIME: 25 minutes

Fancy Bean Substitutes: Flageolet, European Solider, Vallarta, Alubia Blanca

Pumpkin White Bean Chowder

▶ SOY-FREE OPTION* ▶ GLUTEN-FREE ▶ OIL-FREE

Substitute summer squash chunks for the butternut squash to make this delightful soup in the summer. You can also use kale or collards in place of the Swiss chard. You can even add an extra 1½ cups (269 g) whole cooked beans to make it heartier. Serve topped with shredded vegan cheddar, extra vegan sour cream, and/or chopped chives for the whole chowder experience.

½ cup (123 g) pumpkin purée

1 medium potato, diced (peeled if not organic)

2 cloves garlic, minced

1 cup (164 g) corn kernels, fresh or frozen

1½ cups (269 g) cooked white beans or 1 can (15 ounces, or 425 g), rinsed and drained

2 sprigs fresh thyme or 1 teaspoon dried

1 bay leaf

1 cube veggie bouillon

4 cups (950 ml) water

Cayenne or chipotle powder

½ cup (115 g) nondairy sour cream *or Cashew Cream (page 28)

1 cup (235 ml) unsweetened nondairy milk (*use soy-free)

Salt and pepper, to taste

::

YIELD: 4 servings

PER 1½-CUP (355 ML) SERVING: 253.1 calories; 7.2 g total fat; 3.3 g saturated fat; 9.0 g protein; 41.2 g carbohydrate; 8.2 g dietary fiber; 0 mg cholesterol.

TOTAL PREP TIME: 20 minutes

TOTAL COOKING TIME: 20 minutes for stove top, 6 to 8 hours for slow cooker

STOVE-TOP DIRECTIONS

Add everything except the salt and pepper to a large saucepan and cook over medium heat, uncovered, for about 20 minutes to allow the flavors to meld.

Add salt and pepper to taste and remove the thyme stems and bay leaf before serving.

If you want a thicker soup, you can transfer one-third of the soup to a blender or food processor, purée it, and then mix it back into the soup.

SLOW COOKER DIRECTIONS

The night before: Cut up the veggies. Thaw the pumpkin purée if frozen. Store together in one bowl in the fridge.

In the morning: Add everything except the nondairy milk, nondairy sour cream, salt, and pepper. Cook on low for 6 to 8 hours or on high for 3 to 4 hours.

Remove the bay leaf and thyme stems and then add the nondairy milk and sour cream. Thoroughly mix them into the soup. Taste and add salt, pepper, more cayenne, or more thyme if needed.

Fancy Bean Substitute: Hutterite, Lila, Flageolet

Cream of the Crop Garden Soup

▶ SOY-FREE OPTION* ▶ GLUTEN-FREE ▶ OIL-FREE OPTION**

This is a great soup to make at the end of spring when the Swiss chard still looks good and the first ears of corn are starting to show up at the farmers' market.

2 tablespoons (28 ml) olive oil (**use water or broth)

½ small onion, minced

2 cloves garlic, minced

½ red bell pepper

1½ cups (246 g) corn kernels, fresh or frozen

1 medium potato, diced (peeled if not organic)

2 medium carrots, diced (peeled if not organic)

4 cups (950 ml) water

2 bouillon cubes or 3 Easy Veggie Bouillon ice cubes (page 20)

One 2-inch (5 cm) piece lemon zest

¼ teaspoon ground rosemary or ½ teaspoon chopped fresh

1 teaspoon dried thyme or 1 tablespoon (2.4 g) fresh

1 teaspoon dried basil or 1 tablespoon (2.5 g) fresh

2 cups (475 ml) unsweetened nondairy milk (*use soy-free)

1½ cups (269 g) cooked white beans or 1 can (15 ounces, or 425 g), rinsed and drained

1 cup (36 g) chopped Swiss chard

2 cups (240 g) diced summer squash

Salt and pepper, to taste

Heat the oil over medium heat in a large saucepan, add the onion, and cook until soft and translucent, 5 to 7 minutes. Add the garlic and bell pepper and cook for 2 to 3 minutes more.

Add the corn, potato, carrots, water, bouillon, lemon zest, rosemary, thyme, and basil. Bring almost to a boil, decrease the heat to a simmer, and cook until the potato is just tender, about 30 minutes.

Meanwhile, add 1 cup (235 ml) of the nondairy milk and white beans to a blender and blend until smooth. Add the blended mixture to the soup with the remaining 1 cup (235 ml) milk, Swiss chard, and summer squash. Cook until the squash is tender, about 10 to 15 minutes. I like mine to still be a bit firm.

Taste and season with salt and pepper. Also add more herbs if needed.

Fancy Bean Substitutes: Flageolet, European Solider, Vallarta, Alubia Blanca

YIELD: 6 servings

PER 1½-CUP (355 ML) SERVING: 194.4 calories; 7.2 g total fat; 2.4 g saturated fat; 6.7 g protein; 28.1 g carbohydrate; 7.1 g dietary fiber; 0 mg cholesterol.

TOTAL PREP TIME: 20 minutes

TOTAL COOKING TIME: 30 minutes

Salsa Fresca White Bean Gazpacho

▶ SOY-FREE ▶ GLUTEN-FREE ▶ OIL-FREE OPTION*

All you need is a can of beans on hand and you can make this cooling soup on the hottest day without heating up your kitchen!

FOR THE SOUP BASE

6 cups (1.1 kg) fresh chopped tomatoes, in large chunks

½ large bell pepper, cored, seeded, and cut into large chunks

2 tablespoons (20 g) chopped onion

2 cloves garlic

2 tablespoons (28 ml) balsamic vinegar

1 tablespoon (15 ml) olive oil (*omit)

⅓ teaspoon chili powder

Salt, to taste

FOR THE SALSA FRESCA

½ cup (90 g) minced tomato

⅓ bell pepper, cored, seeded, and minced

2 tablespoons (20 g) minced onion

Juice of 2 limes

½ teaspoon chili powder

½ teaspoon salt or to taste

1½ cups (269 g) cooked white beans or 1 can (15 ounces, or 425 g), rinsed and drained

1 small cucumber, chopped (peeled if waxed)

Handful of chopped fresh cilantro

Freshly ground pepper, to taste

To make the soup base, combine all the ingredients in a blender. Purée, taste, and season with salt.

To make the salsa fresca, combine all the ingredients in a bowl.

Pour one-fourth of the soup base into a bowl. Top with one-fourth of the salsa fresca, and one-fourth of the beans. Sprinkle on the cucumber and cilantro. Top with ground pepper.

Fancy Bean Substitutes: Flageolet, European Solider, Vallarta, Alubia Blanca

::

YIELD: 4 servings

PER 1½-CUP (355 ML) SERVING: 217.6 calories; 4.3 g total fat; 0.6 g saturated fat; 11.0 g protein; 37.4 g carbohydrate; 8.1 g dietary fiber; 0 mg cholesterol.

TOTAL PREP TIME: 20 minutes

Triple Lentil Soup with Wheat Berries

▶ SOY-FREE ▶ GLUTEN-FREE OPTION* ▶ OIL-FREE OPTION**

Wheat berries are low-maintenance when you use the slow cooker method, but if you don't feel like bothering, use your favorite quick-cooking whole grain instead!

½ cup (96 g) wheat berries (*use quinoa or millet)

2 tablespoons (28 ml) olive oil (**use water or broth)

½ onion or 1 small leek, minced

3 cloves garlic, minced

½ cup (96 g) brown lentils or green French lentils

½ cup (96 g) petite golden lentils (also called split moong beans)

½ cup (96 g) red lentils

6 cups (1.4 L) water

1 bay leaf

3 whole black cardamom pods

2 cups minced greens (spinach [60 g] or kale [72 g] work great)

Salt (try smoked salt) and pepper, to taste

: :

YIELD: 4 to 6 servings

PER 1½-CUP (355 ML) SERVING: 251.8 calories; 5.2 g total fat; 0.7 g saturated fat; 11.5 g protein; 35.7 g carbohydrate; 9.8 g dietary fiber; 0 mg cholesterol.

TOTAL PREP TIME: 15 minutes

TOTAL COOKING TIME: 60 to 75 minutes for stove top, 8 to 10 hours for slow cooker

STOVE-TOP DIRECTIONS

The night before: Add the wheat berries to a bowl, cover with water, and keep in the fridge until you begin making dinner the next night. (If you are using the optional millet or quinoa, you do not need to presoak.)

The next day: In a medium saucepan, warm the oil over medium heat, add the onion, and sauté until translucent, about 5 minutes. Add the garlic and cook 1 minute more.

Add all the lentils, wheat berries, water, bay leaf, and black cardamom pods to the sautéed mixture in the saucepan. Increase the heat to high and cook until it almost boils, then decrease the heat to low and cook until the wheat berries and lentils are done, 45 to 60 minutes.

Add greens and cook until wilted, about 10 minutes. Remove the bay leaf and cardamom pods. Season with salt and pepper.

SLOW COOKER DIRECTIONS

Heat the oil in a sauté pan over medium heat, add the onion, and sauté until translucent, about 5 minutes. Add the garlic and sauté for 1 minute more.

Add the cooked mixture to a slow cooker along with all the lentils, wheat berries, water, bay leaf, and black cardamom pods. Cook on low for 8 to 10 hours.

Add the greens 30 minutes before serving so as not to overcook them. Remove the bay leaf and cardamom pods. Season with salt and pepper.

Did You Know?

Black and green cardamom are related but black cardamom is dried over an open fire to give it a smoky flavor. If you can't find black cardamom, use the green and liquid smoke, smoked paprika, or smoked salt.

5

COOL BEANS

Legume-Centric Salads

Beans and salads are natural partners. You'll love them in the Asian slaw, rice noodle salad, and my favorite, Indian Chickpea Yogurt Salad.

Marinated White Bean Niçoise Salad

▶ SOY-FREE OPTION* ▶ GLUTEN-FREE

This is a great make-ahead picnic salad. Keep the marinated beans in one container, the potato salad in another, and have the lettuce ready in a bag.

FOR THE MARINATED BEANS

1½ cups (269 g) cooked white beans or 1 can (15 ounces, or 425 g), rinsed and drained

2 to 3 tablespoons (28 to 45 ml) olive oil

2 tablespoons (28 ml) apple cider vinegar

1 teaspoon Dijon mustard

¼ to ½ teaspoon agave nectar

Salt and pepper

FOR THE VEGGIE-POTATO SALAD

12 baby Yellow Finn or red potatoes, cut into quarters (peeled if not organic)

2 carrots, thickly sliced (peeled if not organic)

2 cups (200 g) green beans, ends removed and cut in half

12 olives, pitted and chopped

2 teaspoons herbes de Provence

2 tablespoons (28 g) vegan mayonnaise (*use soy-free)

½ to 1 teaspoon kala namak

Black pepper, to taste

8 cups (440 g) torn lettuce, for serving

....

YIELD: 4 servings

PER SERVING: 602.6 calories; 17.0 g total fat; 1.0 g saturated fat; 16.0 g protein; 104.0 g carbohydrate; 14.8 g dietary fiber; 0 mg cholesterol.

TOTAL PREP TIME: 15 minutes

TOTAL COOKING TIME: 30 minutes

To make the marinated beans, the day or night before, combine all the ingredients in a container that has a tight sealing lid. Shake to get the marinade on all of the beans. Store in the fridge overnight. (It will work if you marinate it for just 30 minutes if you are in a hurry.)

To make the veggie-potato salad, boil the potatoes and carrots in a pot of water until just done, about 20 minutes. Steam the green beans until they are bright green, about 10 to 15 minutes. Once the veggies are cool, add them to a mixing bowl along with the olives, herbs de Provence, and mayonnaise and stir to combine. Stir in the kala namak. This is a salt that smells and tastes like eggs (in a good way), but if you are on a low-sodium diet, feel free to use less. You want to use enough salt to taste the egg flavor. Add the pepper to suit your taste. Store the mixture in the fridge until you are ready to serve.

When ready to serve, place a layer of lettuce on each plate, top with a large scoop of the salad mixture, and sprinkle the beans around and on top.

Did You Know?

• Herbes de Provence is a mixture of thyme, savory, marjoram, rosemary, and lavender flowers. Now you can make some of your own!

• Kala namak is a salt that's used in Indian cooking. It's the ingredient that transforms plain tofu into the perfect breakfast scramble and gives the extra flavor boost to this salad that a nonvegan Nicoise salad gets from eggs.

Fancy Bean Substitutes: Flageolet, Lila, Christmas Limas

Asian Black Soybean Slaw

▶ SOY-FREE OPTION* ▶ GLUTEN-FREE OPTION**

This simple salad has a complex flavor because of the sesame oil, ginger, and sriracha—an Asian hot chili sauce—in the dressing. The best thing is that it takes just a few minutes to make.

1 large head napa cabbage, shredded or chopped small

2 large carrots, grated (peeled if not organic)

2 stalks celery, minced

1 cup (172 g) cooked black soy beans or 1 can (15 ounces, or 425 g), rinsed and drained (*use chickpeas or other non-soy bean)

FOR THE DRESSING

½ cup (120 ml) sesame oil

¼ cup (60 g) rice vinegar

1 tablespoon (8 g) grated fresh ginger

1 tablespoon (15 ml) soy sauce (use *coconut aminos or **gluten-free soy sauce)

1 teaspoon sriracha (**use gluten-free)

:::

YIELD: 4 servings

PER HEAPING 2-CUP (455 G) SERVING: 354.3 calories; 31.4 g total fat; 4.5 g saturated fat; 8.9 g protein; 14.3 g carbohydrate; 5.0 g dietary fiber; 0 mg cholesterol.

TOTAL PREP TIME: 15 minutes

Combine the veggies and beans in a large salad bowl.

To make the dressing, in a small bowl, mix all the ingredients together. Pour over the salad and toss. Store in the fridge for up to 3 days.

Serving Suggestions & Variations

Add other farmers' market veggies and cut them small. I like to use snow peas, bean sprouts, and bell peppers. You can also top this salad with tofu or a crispy chickpea patty to make it a heartier meal.

Fancy Bean Substitutes: Edamame, Ayocote Negro

Pesto White Bean Salad

▶ SOY-FREE ▶ GLUTEN-FREE ▶ OIL-FREE OPTION*

Turn your extra greens into a delicious pesto salad. It's a great way to switch things up in the spring when your fridge is filled with greens. Please note that collards are less bitter after they go through a freeze. If you use them before a freeze, you will need to adjust the other ingredients to balance their bitter flavor.

FOR THE DRESSING

1 cup (36 g) fresh greens (collards, kale, arugula, etc.)

¼ cup (30 g) pecans or walnuts

3 tablespoons (45 ml) orange juice

3 tablespoons (45 ml) water

2 tablespoons (28 ml) olive oil (*use water)

1 tablespoon (6 g) nutritional yeast

½ teaspoon balsamic vinegar (a citrus balsamic is a plus but regular is fine)

Salt, to taste

3 cups (537 g) cooked white beans or 2 cans (15 ounces, or 425 g each), rinsed and drained

2 cups (360 g) chopped tomatoes

8 cups (440 g) lettuce, for serving

::

YIELD: 4 servings

PER SERVING: 296 calories; 12.9 g total fat; 1.4 g saturated fat; 12.5 g protein; 37.9 g carbohydrate; 12.8 g dietary fiber; 0 mg cholesterol.

TOTAL PREP TIME: 10 minutes

To make the dressing, combine all the ingredients except the salt in a food processor and blend until smooth but not completely puréed. It's nice to have a few small bits of nuts for texture. Taste and add salt and more nutritional yeast or orange juice, if desired.

Combine the white beans and tomatoes in a bowl. Pour the dressing over and mix well. You can also add the lettuce to coat the leaves with the dressing or serve the dressed beans on a bed of plain lettuce.

Fancy Bean Substitutes: Cannellini, Flageolet, Christmas Lima

Salsa Quinoa Salad

▶ SOY-FREE ▶ GLUTEN-FREE ▶ OIL-FREE OPTION*

Switch up this salad by using different salsas. You can make it as mild or as spicy as you want. You can even use the Simple Pantry Salsa (page 21).

1 cup (173 g) quinoa, rinsed

2 cups (475 ml) water

1½ cups (266 g) cooked kidney beans or 1 can (15 ounces, or 425 g), rinsed and drained

1½ cups (258 g) cooked black beans or 1 can (15 ounces, or 425 g), rinsed and drained

1½ cups (256 g) cooked pinto beans or 1 can (15 ounces, or 425 g), rinsed and drained

2 summer squash, peeled and diced

1 large green bell pepper, cored, seeded, and diced

1 teaspoon chili powder

1 teaspoon ground cumin

1 cup (250 g) salsa

¼ cup (60 ml) olive oil (*omit oil and use extra salsa)

Juice of 1 lime

½ to 1 cup (8 to 16 g) chopped cilantro

½ teaspoon salt

:::

YIELD: 6 servings

PER SERVING: 391.9 calories; 11.6 g total fat; 1.6 g saturated fat; 15.8 g protein; 58.2 g carbohydrate; 16.0 g dietary fiber; 0 mg cholesterol.

TOTAL PREP TIME: 20 minutes

TOTAL COOKING TIME: 30 minutes

In a saucepan, add the quinoa and water and bring almost to a boil. Decrease the heat to low and cook for 25 to 30 minutes until the tails unravel on the quinoa. It's a signal that they are ready.

While the quinoa is cooking, add the beans, summer squash, and green pepper to a large mixing bowl.

In a smaller bowl, combine the chili powder, cumin, salsa, oil, lime juice, cilantro, and salt. Please note that you can substitute extra salsa for the olive oil if you want to keep it fat-free.

Pour the dressing over the bean mixture and stir to combine. Once the quinoa is done and completely cooled, add it to the bowl and mix again.

Serving Suggestions & Variations

Serve in lettuce or collard wraps.

Fancy Bean Substitutes: Black Calypso, Good Mother Stallard, Cranberry

Indian Chickpea Yogurt Salad

▶ GLUTEN-FREE ▶ OIL-FREE ▶ SOY-FREE OPTION*

My favorite Indian restaurant serves this in the summer, and it can be easily veganized by using soy or coconut yogurt. It's a perfect meal when it's hard to imagine cooking in the heat. Boil the potatoes in the early morning or late at night and keep them in the fridge until dinnertime. This salad can be served on its own or on a bed of lettuce.

3 cups (492 g) cooked chickpeas or 2 cans (15 ounces, or 425 g each), rinsed and drained

1 large potato, cooked and diced (peeled if not organic)

1 large cucumber, diced (peeled if waxed)

½ small onion, minced (optional)

FOR THE DRESSING

1 cup (230 g) unsweetened soy yogurt (*use plain coconut yogurt)

Juice of ½ lime

1½ to 2½ teaspoons kala namak

1½ teaspoons ground cumin

1 teaspoon garlic powder or 1 clove garlic, minced

½ to 1½ teaspoons cayenne or other spicy chili powder

½ teaspoon coriander

Chopped cilantro, for serving

In a large bowl, combine the beans, potato, cucumber, and onion.

To make the dressing, combine all the ingredients in a small bowl. Taste and adjust the seasonings as needed.

Add the dressing to the veggies and mix until thoroughly combined. Serve topped with cilantro.

Serving Suggestions & Variations

• Substitute just about any cooked beans that you have in the fridge, though kidneys and chickpeas tend to keep their shape the best. Add shredded or chopped carrots, summer squash, or even a few spicy radish slices to make it a dish all your own.

• You can leave out the potato if you don't want anything that heavy. I know that some summer days in North Carolina have me just sipping smoothies for dinner!

:::

YIELD: 6 servings

PER SCANT 1½-CUP (340 G)SERVING: 246.4 calories; 2.9 g total fat; 0.2 g saturated fat; 10.2 g protein; 45.6 g carbohydrate; 7.6 g dietary fiber; 0 mg cholesterol.

TOTAL PREP TIME: 20 minutes (including precooking the potato)

Vietnamese Rice Noodle Salad (Bun)

▶ OIL-FREE ▶ SOY-FREE OPTION* ▶ GLUTEN-FREE OPTION**

In this refreshing summer salad "bun" refers to the rice vermicelli and not a traditional wheat bun. But where are the beans/legumes? They're in the sprouts, the sauce, and even the peanut topping!

1 package (6.75 ounces, or 191 g) rice vermicelli (mai fun)

½ cup (75 g) peanuts, minced (optional)

FOR THE DRESSING

½ cup (120 ml) soy sauce (use *coconut aminos or **gluten-free soy sauce)

¼ cup (60 ml) rice vinegar

Juice and zest of 2 limes

2 cloves garlic, minced

2 teaspoons agave nectar

1 teaspoon tamarind paste (optional)

FOR THE SALAD

6 cups (330 g) chopped lettuce

6 cups (624 g) bean sprouts

3 medium cucumbers, peeled and chopped

3 medium carrots, grated (peeled if not organic)

1 cup (16 g) fresh cilantro, chopped

1 cup (40 g) basil, chopped

::

YIELD: 6 servings

PER 3-CUP (675 G) SERVING: 674 calories; 3.7 g total fat; 0.6 g saturated fat; 11.8 g protein; 150.1 g carbohydrate; 7.1 g dietary fiber; 9.3 mg cholesterol.

TOTAL PREP TIME: 25 minutes

TOTAL COOKING TIME: 10 minutes

Cook the rice vermicelli according to the package directions. Drain and run under cool water.

To make the dressing, combine all the ingredients. I like to put them in a mason jar and shake until they're mixed.

To make the salad, divide the lettuce among 6 bowls and top each equally with vermicelli, bean sprouts, cucumber, carrot, cilantro, and basil. Serve with a small dish of dressing (about ¼ cup [60 ml]) for each diner. Top with minced peanuts if desired.

Did You Know?

People avoid gluten for many different reasons. But be aware that some people do it for medical reasons and can get very sick if the food has come into contact with gluten at the factory or even on your cutting board. If you are not gluten-free yourself, make sure to check labels for any warnings before you serve them to people who don't eat gluten. I'm sure your gluten-free friends will be glad to answer any questions you have, after all you are making them dinner!

Lentil Beet Salad

▶ SOY-FREE OPTION* ▶ GLUTEN-FREE
▶ OIL-FREE

Beets and lentils come together perfectly in this creamy salad. Serve plain or over mixed greens.

3 cups (675 g) peeled and chopped beets

¾ cup (144 g) lentils

1½ cups (355 ml) water

FOR THE DRESSING

1 cup (230 g) unsweetened vegan yogurt (*use soy-free)

Juice and zest of 1 lemon

1 teaspoon tarragon

1 teaspoon thyme

1 teaspoon basil

½ teaspoon Dijon mustard

½ teaspoon agave nectar

Salt and pepper, to taste

Place the beets in a saucepan, cover with water, bring to a boil, and then cover and simmer until they can be pierced with a fork, 20 to 30 minutes.

In another saucepan, add the lentils and water. Bring to a boil, and then cover and simmer until the lentils are tender, 20 to 30 minutes. Rinse under cool water.

Add beets and lentils to a large bowl.

To make the dressing, mix all the ingredients together. Toss with the beet-lentil mixture.

YIELD: 6 servings

PER ¾-CUP (170 G) SERVING: 165.4 calories; 1.2 g total fat; 0 g saturated fat; 7.9 g protein; 29.2 g carbohydrate; 6.2 g dietary fiber; 0 mg cholesterol.

TOTAL PREP TIME: 20 minutes

TOTAL COOKING TIME: 30 minutes

Christmas Lima and Bulgur Salad ▶

▶ SOY-FREE ▶ GLUTEN-FREE OPTION*

Christmas lima beans are like no other bean. They have a firm texture and an almost chestnutlike flavor.

2 cups (475 ml) water

1 cup (140 g) bulgur (*use quinoa [173 g], millet [200 g], or amaranth [208 g])

2 veggie bouillon cubes

3 cups (510 g) cooked Christmas lima beans, kidney beans, or chickpeas or 2 cans (15 ounces, or 425 g each), rinsed and drained

Zest of 1 lemon

FOR THE DRESSING

¼ cup (60 ml) olive oil

Juice of 1 lemon

1 clove garlic, minced

½ teaspoon smoked salt

Black pepper, to taste

Bring the water to a boil in a saucepan. Add bulgur and bouillon, stir, cover, remove from heat, and let sit for 15 to 20 minutes.

Combine the cooked bulgur, beans, and lemon zest in a large salad bowl.

To make the dressing, combine all the ingredients, then pour over the salad and toss. Taste and adjust salt or lemon juice if needed.

YIELD: 4 servings

PER SERVING: 461.6 calories; 15.3 g total fat; 2.1 g saturated fat; 17.0 g protein; 64.8 g carbohydrate; 16.3 g dietary fiber; 0 mg cholesterol.

TOTAL PREP TIME: 20 minutes

TOTAL COOKING TIME: 10 minutes

Chickpea Greek Salad with Tofu Feta

▶ GLUTEN-FREE ▶ OIL-FREE

This is a recipe that has summer on its mind. If you have some cooked chickpeas in the fridge or a can in the pantry for emergencies, you don't have to cook anything!

FOR THE TOFU FETA

1 package (15.5 ounces, or 439 g) tofu, pressed, cut into small cubes

¼ cup (60 ml) lemon juice

Zest of 1 lemon

½ teaspoon each salt and oregano

FOR THE SIMPLE YOGURT DRESSING

1 cup (230 g) unsweetened vegan yogurt

2 cloves garlic, minced

2 teaspoons lemon juice

1 teaspoon apple cider vinegar

Salt and pepper, to taste

FOR THE SALAD

1½ cups (246 g) cooked chickpeas or 1 can (15 ounces, or 425 g), rinsed and drained

1 large head romaine lettuce, chopped

3 small tomatoes, chopped

1 large cucumber, chopped (peeled if waxed)

½ bell pepper, cored, and chopped

½ cup (80 g) chopped red onion

½ cup (85 g) pitted kalamata olives

Handful of fresh parsley, chopped

1 to 2 tablespoons (4 to 8 g) minced fresh oregano (optional)

To make the tofu feta, combine all the ingredients in a container that has a tightly sealing lid. Shake to get the marinade on all of the tofu. I also like to turn it over in the container a few times while I'm making the salad to get the lemony goodness into every piece of tofu. You can make this the day before and let it marinate longer in the fridge.

To make the dressing, mix all the ingredients in a small bowl and set aside. Again you can make this in advance and keep in the fridge.

To make the salad, combine all the ingredients in a large salad bowl and mix gently. Add the dressing and toss. This will coat all the veggies evenly and make for a better salad experience. You actually use less dressing when you toss the salad than when you pour it over the top. Or serve it on the side.

Crumble the tofu feta over the top. You can garnish with extra olives or sprigs of parsley.

YIELD: 4 servings

PER SERVING: 405.7 calories; 16.3 g total fat; 0.2 g saturated fat; 19.9 g protein; 44.4 g carbohydrate; 9.1 g dietary fiber; 0 mg cholesterol.

TOTAL PREP TIME: 20 minutes

6

PORTABLE BEANS

Sandwiches, Patties, and More

Sandwiches can be a nutritious foundation of a busy life. Keeping a few pupusas and burritos in the freezer for a last-minute dinner is a great thing to do and keeps your budget in order. Recipes like the Sloppy Buffalo Beans or Mango Curry Chickpea Salad take almost no time to make but are incredibly flavorful. Be sure to try the spreads from the noshing chapter slathered on your favorite bread for a quick dinner, too.

Sloppy Buffalo Beans

▶ SOY-FREE OPTION* ▶ OIL-FREE OPTION** ▶ GLUTEN-FREE OPTION***

This is a Sloppy Joe variation and a little spicy. If your family isn't a fan of heat, use less hot sauce or a milder sauce in its place.

FOR THE RANCH DRESSING

½ cup (115 g) unsweetened vegan yogurt (*use soy-free)

3 tablespoons vegan mayonnaise (*use soy-free or **use oil-free mayo substitute)

Juice of ½ lemon

1 teaspoon agave

½ teaspoon garlic powder or 1 clove garlic, minced

½ teaspoon thyme

½ teaspoon salt

¼ teaspoon each ground black pepper, smoked paprika, and onion powder

3 cups (531 g) cooked kidney beans or 2 cans (15 ounces, or 425 g each), rinsed and drained

¼ to ½ cup (60 to 120 ml) cayenne pepper sauce or Buffalo hot sauce

2 tablespoons (32 g) tomato paste

1 teaspoon thyme

¼ to ½ teaspoon liquid smoke

1 clove garlic, minced

½ cup (115 g) vegan sour cream *or Cashew Cream (page 28)

4 whole wheat buns, lightly toasted (***use gluten-free)

Minced carrot and celery, for serving

To make the dressing, mix all the ingredients and store in the fridge until ready to serve.

Add the kidney beans, hot sauce, tomato paste, thyme, liquid smoke, and garlic to a saucepan and cook over medium heat until the garlic mellows, about 5 to 10 minutes. Add the sour cream and heat thoroughly.

Serve over the toasted buns open-face style topped with the carrot and celery mixture and the ranch dressing. If you have some unexpected guests, serve as a regular sandwich and the filling will stretch up to eight sandwiches.

Fancy Bean Substitutes: Vaquero, Borlotti

::

YIELD: 4 servings

PER SERVING: 519.9 calories; 12.0 g total fat; 2.5 g saturated fat; 22.9 g protein; 81.5 g carbohydrate; 16.6 g dietary fiber; 0 mg cholesterol.

TOTAL PREP TIME: 20 minutes

TOTAL COOKING TIME: 10 to 15 minutes

Hawaiian Sliders

▶ OIL-FREE ▶ OIL-FREE OPTION**

These sliders have pineapple, ginger, and hoisin sauce in addition to mushrooms, kidney beans, rice, and bread crumbs. Party food at its best!

1½ cups (293 g) cooked cold brown rice

1½ cups (266 g) cooked kidney beans or 1 can (15 ounces, or 425 g), rinsed and drained

1 cup (70 g) minced mushrooms

1 cup (115 g) whole wheat bread crumbs

½ cup (120 g) crushed pineapple, drained

⅓ cup (50 g) minced bell pepper

1 tablespoon (16 g) tomato paste

1 tablespoon (15 ml) vegan Worcestershire sauce

1 teaspoon hoisin sauce

1 teaspoon smoked paprika

½ to 1 teaspoon sriracha

½ teaspoon each ground ginger and garlic powder

¼ teaspoon onion powder

Salt and pepper, to taste

FOR THE SLIDER SAUCE

⅓ cup (80 g) crushed pineapple

2 tablespoons (30 g) ketchup

1 tablespoon (16 g) hoisin sauce

½ teaspoon sriracha

36 mini whole wheat rolls

Preheat the oven to 400°F (200°C, or gas mark 6) and oil 2 sheet pans **or line with parchment paper.

Process the brown rice in a food processor. If it is not cold it will become mush, but if it's cold it will be cut into tiny bits.

In a large mixing bowl, smash the beans with a fork or pastry cutter. Then add the rice and the rest of the ingredients and mix. Use a small cookie scoop to scoop out the mixture and place on the sheet pan and then press them down with your fingers to make them thinner. Cook on one side for 12 minutes, flip, and cook on the other side for 10 minutes.

To make the sauce, combine all the ingredients together in a small food processor.

Serve the sliders topped with the sauce on mini whole wheat rolls.

:::

YIELD: 36 sliders and ½ cup (125 g) sauce

PER SLIDER PATTY (WITH SAUCE): 37.8 calories; 0.2 g total fat; 0 g saturated fat; 1.3 g protein; 7.6 g carbohydrate; 1.2 g dietary fiber; 0 mg cholesterol.

TOTAL PREP TIME: 20 minutes

TOTAL COOKING TIME: 22 minutes

Mango Curry Chickpea Salad

▶ SOY-FREE ▶ GLUTEN-FREE ▶ OIL-FREE

This is a tasty mango twist on the obligatory mock tuna salad sandwich. If your mango is a bit dry, feel free to add a teaspoon or two of unsweetened vegan yogurt or vegan mayonnaise.

1½ cups (246 g) cooked chickpeas or 1 can (15 ounces, or 425 g), rinsed and drained

½ cup (90 g) minced fresh mango

1 teaspoon grated fresh ginger

1 teaspoon minced cilantro

¼ teaspoon garam masala

Salt, to taste

Put the chickpeas in a bowl and mash with a fork, leaving them slightly chunky. Mix in the rest of the ingredients. Serve in a pita with avocado slices, on a cold sandwich, or in an open-faced tunalike melt with vegan cheese lightly toasted in the oven.

YIELD: 2 cups (450 g)

PER ½-CUP (112 G) SERVING: 115.3 calories; 1.6 g total fat; 0.2 g saturated fat; 5.4 g protein; 16.9 g carbohydrate; 4.8 g dietary fiber; 0 mg cholesterol.

TOTAL PREP TIME: 15 minutes

Grilled Almond Cheez with Figs

▶ SOY-FREE ▶ GLUTEN-FREE OPTION*
▶ OIL-FREE OPTION**

This is a tasty way to use the Almond Cheez Spread from the appetizer chapter.

¼ cup (62 g) Almond Cheez Spread (page 54)

2 slices whole grain bread (*use gluten-free)

1 fresh fig, sliced, or 2 tablespoons (40 g) fig jam

Vegan margarine or olive oil (**omit)

Heat a sauté pan or panini pan over medium heat. Spread the cheez on one slice of the bread, top with the sliced figs, and second slice of bread.

If you have a nonstick pan, you can grill it dry. Or spread about 1 teaspoon of margarine on each side. (Alternatively, you can spritz each side with a little olive oil.)

If you have a panini press, place the sandwich in the hot pan and top with the heavy press to flatten it. If not, take a smaller heavy skillet and use it as a press.

Cook on one side until it turns golden brown, about 3 to 5 minutes, flip, and press on the other side for about 3 to 5 more minutes.

YIELD: 1 serving

PER SERVING: 413.5 calories; 13.2 g total fat; 2.1 g saturated fat; 11.5 g protein; 47.6 g carbohydrate; 7.4 g dietary fiber; 0.2 mg cholesterol.

TOTAL PREP TIME: 10 minutes

TOTAL COOKING TIME: 10 minutes

Black Bean Salvadoran Tortillas (Pupusas)

▶ SOY-FREE ▶ GLUTEN-FREE ▶ OIL-FREE OPTION*

These are Salvadoran stuffed tortillas. They have a strong corn taste from the masa, a ground corn flour treated with lime, and a spicy center. You can skip the bean filling and use vegan cheese in the middle, but this *is* a bean book, after all.

FOR THE BEAN FILLING

2 tablespoons (28 ml) olive oil (*use water or broth)

½ onion, minced

2 cloves garlic, minced

¾ teaspoon chili powder

½ teaspoon oregano

¼ teaspoon cumin

¼ teaspoon chipotle powder

1½ cups (258 g) cooked black beans or 1 can (15 oz or 425 g), rinsed and drained

FOR THE DOUGH

2½ cups (290 g) masa

2 cups (475 ml) water

½ teaspoon salt

Salsa, store-bought or homemade (page 21), for serving

:::

YIELD: 12 pupusas

PER PUPUSA: 135.8 calories; 3.2 g total fat; 0.3 g saturated fat; 3.7 g protein; 23.3 g carbohydrate; 3.3 g dietary fiber; 0 mg cholesterol.

TOTAL PREP TIME: 40 minutes

TOTAL COOKING TIME: 20 minutes

To make the filling, heat the oil in a sauté pan and cook the onion until translucent, about 5 minutes. Add the garlic and spices and sauté for 1 minute more.

Add the beans and sauté while smashing a few of them with a wooden spoon. Set aside to cool.

Preheat the oven to 350°F (180°C, or gas mark 4) and oil 2 sheet pans *or line with parchment paper.

To make the dough, add all the ingredients to a mixing bowl and stir to combine. Take a piece of the dough and make a small ball. The edges of the ball should not crack when flattened; if they do, add more water to the batter.

To make the pupusas, first make 12 slightly bigger than golf ball–size balls (about 2 tablespoons [28 g] each) and set on a cutting board.

Take a ball and smash it down while keeping it thicker than a regular pie crust. Put a heaping teaspoon of the filling in the middle and gently bring the edges together, forming another ball with the filling in the center.

Roll the ball in your hand and try to get the dough to an even thickness surrounding the filling. If you have a thin spot, it will break or crack in the next step.

Lightly smash the ball into a patty using your fingers but avoiding your palms. I find that the dough sticks to my palms and breaks. Place the thick patty on the baking sheet and repeat for each pupusa.

Bake on one side for 10 minutes and then flip and bake for 10 minutes more. Serve topped with salsa.

Fancy Bean Substitutes: Black Calypso, Purple Runner

Don't Be Crabby Cakes

▶ SOY-FREE ▶ OIL-FREE OPTION* ▶ GLUTEN-FREE OPTION**

These are great in a whole wheat bun and can be served at room temperature, so they're handy for picnics.

2 tablespoons (28 ml) olive oil (*use water or broth)

½ small onion, minced

3 cloves garlic, minced

1 green bell pepper, cored, seeded, and minced

3 stalks celery, minced

1 tablespoon (7 g) plus 1 teaspoon Old Bay Seasoning (you can use extra Cajun Spice Blend in a pinch)

1 tablespoon (9 g) plus 1 teaspoon Cajun Spice Blend (page 29)

3 cups (537 g) cooked white beans or 2 cans (15 ounces, or 425 g each), rinsed and drained

2 tablespoons (14 g) ground flaxseed mixed with ¼ cup (60 ml) warm water

½ cup (120 ml) water

½ to 1 cup (33 to 67 g) minced greens (kale, collards, chard, etc.)

3 cups (585 g) cooked brown rice

Salt and pepper, to taste

18 whole wheat buns (**use gluten-free)

Preheat the oven to 350°F (180°C, or gas mark 4). Oil 2 sheet pans *or line with parchment paper.

Heat the olive oil in a large sauté pan over medium heat. Add the onion and sauté until translucent. Add the garlic, green pepper, celery, and spices and cook until the peppers soften.

Put the white beans, flaxseed mixture, and water into a food processor and pulse until the beans are broken up but not puréed. Scrape the contents into a large bowl and add the sautéed veggies, greens, and brown rice. Mix and mash as needed to get the mixture to start sticking together. Add more water if needed, 1 tablespoon (15 ml) at a time. Taste and season with salt and pepper.

Use a large cookie or muffin scoop (one that holds about ¼ cup [55 g]) to make 18 patties on the prepared sheet pan. Slightly flatten the tops with the back of the scoop.

Cook for 30 minutes, carefully flip the patties over, and cook 15 to 25 minutes.

Let the patties cool a little. Serve on a bun topped with the Kohlrabi Slaw. (Plain slaw works just fine, too!)

YIELD: 18 patties

PER PATTY WITH 2 TABLESPOONS (28 G) SLAW: 94.6 calories; 2.2 g total fat; 0.3 g saturated fat; 3.6 g protein; 16.7 g carbohydrate; 3.4 g dietary fiber; 0 mg cholesterol.

TOTAL PREP TIME: 30 minutes

TOTAL COOKING TIME: 45 to 55 minutes

Kohlrabi Slaw

▶ SOY-FREE ▶ GLUTEN-FREE ▶ OIL-FREE

2 large kohlrabi, peeled and grated

½ cup (115 g) unsweetened vegan yogurt

2 teaspoons apple cider vinegar

2 teaspoons agave nectar

Salt and pepper, to taste

Combine all the ingredients in a bowl. Serve!

Crispy Chickpea Patties and Cornbread Waffles

▶ SOY-FREE OPTION* ▶ OIL-FREE

This savory waffle has just a hint of spice that lets it stand up to the tastiest gravy.

FOR THE DRY INGREDIENTS

1½ cups (210 g) cornmeal

½ cup (60 g) whole wheat pastry flour

1 teaspoon baking powder

½ teaspoon baking soda

½ teaspoon salt

½ teaspoon ground cumin

½ teaspoon garlic powder or 1 clove garlic, minced

½ teaspoon smoked paprika

½ teaspoon chili powder

FOR THE WET INGREDIENTS

1½ cups (246 g) cooked chickpeas or 1 can (15 ounces, or 425 g), rinsed and drained

¾ cup (180 ml) unsweetened nondairy milk (*use soy-free)

2 tablespoons (14 g) ground flaxseed mixed with ¼ cup (60 ml) warm water

6 Baked Crispy Chickpea Seitan Patties (page 22)

::

YIELD: 6 Belgian waffles

PER WAFFLE WITH GRAVY: 275.1 calories; 8.4 g total fat; 3.2 g saturated fat; 7.5 g protein; 45.1 g carbohydrate; 11.1 g dietary fiber; 0 mg cholesterol.

TOTAL PREP TIME: 20 minutes

TOTAL COOKING TIME: 10 minutes

To make the waffles, preheat waffle iron.

To prepare the dry ingredients, sift all the ingredients into a large mixing bowl. Set aside.

To prepare the wet ingredients, add the ingredients into a food processor and blend until smooth. Add the wet ingredients to the dry ingredients and combine.

Add the batter to the waffle iron and cook according to instructions.

Place a patty on each waffle and serve with the pepper gravy.

Old-Fashioned Southern Pepper Gravy

▶ SOY-FREE

2 tablespoons (28 g) vegan margarine

3 tablespoons (23 g) flour

2 cups (475 ml) unsweetened coconut milk or other nondairy milk

Salt and pepper, to taste

Melt the margarine in a sauté pan over medium heat. Sprinkle in the flour and whisk, lowering the heat. Cook until the flour starts to take on color. Add the milk and increase the heat to medium-high. Keep whisking until the gravy starts to thicken. Take off the heat just before it has reached your desired thickness. It will still thicken a bit more once you take it off the heat.

Add salt and pepper to taste before serving. Southerners like me add enough black pepper that the gravy gets a little spicy. Of course, you should make it the way your family likes it.

Butternut Squash Frijoles

▶ SOY-FREE ▶ GLUTEN-FREE ▶ OIL-FREE OPTION*

This unusual refried bean variation adds butternut squash to the mix. These are super easy to make in a small slow cooker. The leftovers freeze great as-is or rolled up in burritos.

3 cups (513 g) cooked pinto beans or 2 cans (15 ounces, or 425 g each), rinsed and drained

1 cup (245 g) butternut squash purée

1 tablespoon (15 ml) olive oil (*use water or broth)

1 clove garlic, minced

½ cup (120 ml) water

1 can (14.5 ounces, or 410 g) diced tomatoes or 1½ cups (270 g) chopped fresh

1 teaspoon marjoram

½ teaspoon powdered chipotle or smoked paprika

½ teaspoon chili powder

1 tablespoon (1 g) chopped fresh cilantro

Juice of ½ lime

Salt, to taste

Ground cayenne pepper, to taste

::

YIELD: 6 servings

PER SERVING: 168.5 calories; 3.0 g total fat; 0.8 g saturated fat; 9.2 g protein; 27.4 g carbohydrate; 8.8 g dietary fiber; 0 mg cholesterol.

TOTAL PREP TIME: 20 minutes

TOTAL COOKING TIME: 15 minutes for stove top, 15 to 17 hours for slow cooker

STOVE-TOP DIRECTIONS

Combine the beans and squash in a bowl and mash with a potato masher.

Heat the olive oil in a sauté pan over medium heat. Add the garlic and sauté for about 1 minute and then add the water, tomatoes, marjoram, chipotle, chili powder, and the bean and squash mixture.

Keep mashing as you are cooking the mixture down. The beans will break down more as they cook. You can leave them chunkier if that's the way you prefer them.

Cook until the mixture is combined and heated through, about 15 minutes, and then add the cilantro, lime juice, salt, and cayenne.

SLOW COOKER DIRECTIONS (WITH DRIED BEANS)

The night before: Combine 1 cup (193 g) dried beans and 3 cups (700 ml) water in a 1½- or 2-quart (1.4 or 1.8 L) slow cooker and cook on low overnight or for 8 hours.

In the morning: Add the butternut squash, garlic, water, tomatoes, marjoram, chipotle, and chili powder. Cook on low for 7 to 9 hours.

Taste and adjust the seasonings. Add the cilantro, lime juice, salt, and cayenne.

Fancy Bean Substitutes: Anasazi, Yellow-Eyed Peas, or other soft cooking bean

Where's Dinner? Quick Burrito Filling

▶ SOY-FREE ▶ OIL-FREE OPTION* ▶ GLUTEN-FREE OPTION**

Try using this filling in tacos or on nachos for a weeknight change of pace.

2 tablespoons (28 ml) olive oil (*use water or broth)

½ small onion, minced

2 cloves garlic, minced

½ medium bell pepper, cored, seeded, and chopped

1 jalapeño pepper, seeded and minced (look for mild jalapeños if you don't love spicy food)

1 medium summer squash (yellow, zucchini, etc.), chopped

3 tablespoons (27 g) diced green chiles

1½ teaspoons chili powder

1 teaspoon ground cumin

½ teaspoon chipotle powder (optional)

½ teaspoon salt

½ teaspoon smoked paprika

1 can (14.5 ounces, or 410 g) diced tomatoes or 1½ cups (270 g) chopped fresh

1½ cups (257 g) cooked pinto beans or 1 can (15 ounces, or 425 g), rinsed and drained

1 cup (164 g) corn kernels, fresh or frozen

3 cups (108 g) minced Swiss chard or other green

2 tablespoons (2 g) minced fresh cilantro

8 small burrito tortillas (**use gluten-free)

::

YIELD: 8 burritos, 4 cups (1 kg) filling

PER BURRITO WITH ½ CUP (125 G) FILLING: 270.0 calories; 8.4 g total fat; 2.2 g saturated fat; 9.5 g protein; 43.2 g carbohydrate; 5.5 g dietary fiber; 0 mg cholesterol.

TOTAL PREP TIME: 20 minutes

TOTAL COOKING TIME: 20 minutes

Heat the oil in a large sauté pan over medium heat. Add the onion and sauté until translucent, about 5 minutes. Add the garlic, peppers, squash, green chiles, and spices and sauté for about 5 minutes more until the spices become more aromatic or the pan is starting to get dry and needs liquid.

Add the tomatoes, beans, corn, and Swiss chard. Cover and cook for about 10 minutes and then remove the cover and cook off some of the liquid if it's too watery. Remove from the heat and stir in the cilantro.

If your tortillas are too stiff to bend on their own without breaking, take 2 tortillas and place on top of the mixture in the sauté pan for about 30 seconds or until they get soft enough to roll. Take each off, put on a cutting board with the steamed side up, spread some of the filling inside, and roll up. Repeat until all your burritos are full.

Serving Suggestions & Variations

Any cooked bean you have on hand will work, and the veggies can be switched out to match the seasons.

• **SPRING:** Add in baby turnips and their greens along with carrots in place of the summer squash. You could even use fresh cooked fava beans in place of the pintos if you want to do it up!

• **SUMMER:** Cook up some eggplant and a few mushrooms instead of summer squash and try a new heirloom bean.

• **FALL:** Sweet potatoes and black beans are my fall favorite.

• **WINTER:** This can be a beans and greens extravaganza, and I won't tell if you slip in some of the bok choy that's building up in your fridge.

Baked Arugula and Bean Flautas

▶ SOY-FREE ▶ OIL-FREE OPTION* ▶ GLUTEN-FREE OPTION**

This is a great quick meal. It's even better if you make the bean veggie mixture the night before. Then it only takes a few minutes to pop them in the oven.

1 to 2 tablespoons (15 to 28 ml) olive oil (*use water or broth)

¼ onion, minced

2 cloves garlic, minced

2 small tomatoes, minced

1 cup (20 g) minced arugula or other green

1½ cups (257 g) cooked pinto or black beans or 1 can (15 ounces, or 425 g), rinsed and drained

1 teaspoon marjoram

½ teaspoon salt (smoked or plain)

½ teaspoon chili powder

2 teaspoons minced cilantro

12 taco-size (6-inch, or 15 cm) flour tortillas (**use gluten-free)

::

YIELD: 12 flautas

PER FLAUTA: 177.4 calories; 5.3 g total fat; 1.2 g saturated fat; 5.2 g protein; 27.0 g carbohydrate; 2.3 g dietary fiber; 0 mg cholesterol.

TOTAL PREP TIME: 30 minutes

TOTAL COOKING TIME: 15 to 20 minutes

Preheat the oven to 350°F (180°C, or gas mark 4). Oil a sheet pan *or line with parchment paper.

Heat the oil in a large sauté pan over medium heat. Once hot, add the onion and sauté until translucent, about 5 minutes. Add the garlic and sauté for 1 minute more.

Add the tomatoes, arugula, beans, marjoram, salt, and chili powder. Mash the beans as you are stirring so that they are like refried beans. You can add water as needed if the mixture dries out too much. Stir in the cilantro and remove from the heat.

If your tortillas are too stiff to roll, microwave them for a few seconds. Place a couple of tablespoons (28 g) of the bean mixture in each tortilla, roll up, and put seam side down on the sheet pan. Bake for 15 to 20 minutes until crispy, turning them over about halfway through. The softer your tortillas are, the longer they will take to get crispy.

Serving Suggestions & Variations

No flour tortillas on hand? Use corn tortillas and then they become taquitos!

7

SULTRY STEWS AND HEARTY CHILIS

Quintessential Bean Dishes

International stews are a big hit with my food–loving family and super easy to whip up at the last minute. Don't overlook the deceptively plain beans that, when cooked down with a few veggies and spices, turn into the creamiest delights. You can use cookie cutters to cut out shapes for the grit cakes with the black-eyed peas. I used a ghost cookie cutter for my Halloween dinner last year and everyone loved it!

Chickpea Veggie Tagine

▶ SOY-FREE ▶ OIL-FREE OPTION* ▶ GLUTEN-FREE OPTION**

The name tagine comes from the beautiful clay dish that it's cooked in. It consists of an oven-safe dish that's topped with a tall, cone-shaped lid. It seems like tagines are popping up everywhere lately. But if you, like me, just haven't gotten around to buying one, use a Dutch oven instead.

2 tablespoons (28 ml) olive oil (*use water or broth)

½ small onion, minced

3 cloves garlic, minced

½ bell pepper, cored, seeded, and minced

1½ teaspoons ground coriander

1 teaspoon ground cumin

1 teaspoon smoked paprika

1 teaspoon chili powder

1 teaspoon cardamom

½ teaspoon salt

½ teaspoon cinnamon

1 cup (235 ml) water

2 small carrots, diced (peeled if not organic)

1 small sweet potato, peeled and diced

½ medium head cauliflower, broken into small florets

12 dried apricot halves, minced

3 cups (492 g) cooked chickpeas or 2 cans (15 ounces, or 425 g each), rinsed and drained

3 to 6 cups (471 to 942 g) cooked whole wheat couscous, for serving (**use gluten-free)

··

YIELD: 6 servings

PER 1½-CUP (355 ML) SERVING (DOES NOT INCLUDE COUSCOUS): 210.5 calories; 3.5 g total fat; 0.3 g saturated fat; 9.9 g protein; 39.9 g carbohydrate; 14.9 g dietary fiber; 0 mg cholesterol.

TOTAL PREP TIME: 20 minutes

TOTAL COOKING TIME: 50 to 60 minutes for stove top, 7 to 9 hours for slow cooker

STOVE-TOP DIRECTIONS

Preheat the oven to 350°F (180°C, or gas mark 4). Heat the oil in a large, oven-safe saucepan over medium heat. Add the onion and sauté until translucent, about 5 minutes. Add garlic and bell pepper and sauté for 2 minutes more. Add spices and cook for another minute.

Mix in the rest of the ingredients, except the couscous, cover, and cook in the oven for 45 to 55 minutes or until the sweet potatoes are completely cooked.

Serve over cooked couscous.

SLOW COOKER DIRECTIONS

Heat the oil in a 2-quart (1.8 L) sauté pan over medium heat. Once hot, add the onion and sauté until translucent, about 5 minutes. Then add the garlic and bell pepper and sauté for 2 minutes more. Add the spices and sauté another minute.

Add everything to the slow cooker, except the couscous. Cook on low for 7 to 9 hours.

Serve over cooked couscous.

Fancy Bean Substitutes: Scarlet Runner, Tepary, Good Mother Stallard

Thai Sweet Potato Bean Stew

▶ SOY-FREE ▶ GLUTEN-FREE ▶ OIL-FREE

Beans and sweet potatoes are bathed in rich coconut milk with a little heat from the jalapeño. The best part is being surprised with bursts of flavor from the ginger, lemony herbs, and fresh cilantro. All that and it's easy enough to make after a hard day at work. Serve over rice for a complete meal.

1 large sweet potato, peeled and chopped

3 cups (531 g) cooked kidney beans or (492 g) chickpeas or 2 cans (15 ounces, or 425 g each), rinsed and drained

1 mild jalapeño, seeded and minced

1 cup (235 ml) water

1 can (14 ounces, or 390 ml) light coconut milk

2 cloves garlic, minced

1 tablespoon (8 g) grated fresh ginger

1 cube veggie bouillon

1 tablespoon (5 g) lemon grass, lemon verbena, or lemon balm, minced

½ teaspoon dried ground galanga root (or ¼ teaspoon coriander plus ⅛ teaspoon cayenne)

Zest of ½ lime

Salt, to taste

Fresh cilantro or Thai basil, for serving

:::

YIELD: 4 servings

PER 1½-CUP (355 ML) SERVING (DOES NOT INCLUDE RICE): 255.8 calories; 6.0 g total fat; 5.4 g saturated fat; 10.8 g protein; 38.8 g carbohydrate; 13.4 g dietary fiber; 0 mg cholesterol.

TOTAL PREP TIME: 15 minutes

TOTAL COOKING TIME: 20 to 30 minutes for stove top, 8 to 9 hours for slow cooker

STOVE-TOP DIRECTIONS

Put everything except the salt and cilantro into a soup pot. Bring to a simmer over medium-high heat and then decrease the heat to low. Cook until the potatoes are easily pierced with a fork, 20 to 30 minutes.

Mash a few of the sweet potatoes to thicken up the stew, add salt if needed, and serve over rice. Top with the chopped cilantro.

SLOW COOKER DIRECTIONS

Put everything except the salt and cilantro into a 4-quart (3.8 L) slow cooker. Cook on low for 8 to 9 hours.

Mash a few of the sweet potatoes to thicken up the stew, add salt if needed, and serve over rice. Top with the chopped cilantro.

Did You Know?

Galanga root looks like ginger root, but the flavor is different and actually closer to that of cardamom. It's used in Thai food. If you can't find it in your area, take a look at the Resources Guide, page 185, to find an online source that will deliver it right to your door.

Fancy Bean Substitutes: Ayocote Negro (black runner beans) cook up to be huge, firm black beans that make a wonderful broth. They are perfect in this stew.

Kidney Bean Masala (Rajma)

▶ SOY-FREE ▶ GLUTEN-FREE ▶ OIL-FREE OPTION*

I eat Indian food almost every day. I love the bold flavors and the endless variety. This is a dish you can make on a weeknight if you already have cooked beans, and it works in the slow cooker, too!

2 tablespoons (28 ml) olive oil (*use water or broth)

½ small onion, minced

1 teaspoon ground turmeric

1 teaspoon cumin seeds or ½ teaspoon ground cumin

½ teaspoon coriander seeds or ½ teaspoon ground coriander

½ teaspoon mustard seeds or ¼ teaspoon mustard powder

¼ to ½ teaspoon chili powder

¼ teaspoon ground cinnamon

2 cloves garlic, peeled

1-inch (2.5-cm) piece fresh ginger, sliced

1 to 2 tablespoons (15 to 28 ml) water, as needed

3 cups (531 g) cooked kidney beans or 2 cans (15 ounces, or 410 g each), rinsed and drained

1½ cups (420 g) diced tomatoes or 1 can (14.5 ounces, or 406 g)

¼ to ½ cup (60 to 120 ml) water

Salt, to taste

Chopped fresh cilantro, for garnish

2 to 4 cups (330 to 660 g) cooked rice, for serving

STOVE-TOP DIRECTIONS

To make the curry paste, heat the olive oil over medium heat in a soup pot. Add the onion and sauté until translucent, about 5 minutes, then add the turmeric, cumin, coriander, mustard seeds, chili powder, and cinnamon, and cook for a minute or two more until the spices become more fragrant. Add the cooked mixture and the garlic, ginger, and water to your food processor. Process until minced but still a little chunky.

Add the curry paste, kidney beans, tomatoes, and ¼ cup (60 ml) water to a large pot. Cook over low heat for 30 to 45 minutes or until the tomatoes are broken down. Add more water during cooking as needed.

Taste and add salt to your liking. Garnish with the cilantro. Serve over rice.

SLOW COOKER DIRECTIONS

The night before: Heat olive oil over medium heat in a soup pot. Add onions and sauté until translucent. Add the spices and cook for a minute or two more until the onions become more fragrant. Add the cooked mixture and the rest of the curry paste ingredients into your food processor. Process until minced but still a little chunky.

In the morning: Add the curry paste, kidney beans, tomatoes and ¼ cup (60 ml) water. Cook on low 8 to 10 hours.

....

YIELD: 4 servings

PER 1½-CUP (355 ML) SERVING (DOES NOT INCLUDE RICE): 254.0 calories; 7.5 g total fat; 1.0 g saturated fat; 11.2 g protein; 36.0 g carbohydrate; 13.5 g dietary fiber; 0 mg cholesterol.

TOTAL PREP TIME: 20 minutes

TOTAL COOKING TIME: 30 to 45 minutes for stove top, 8 to 10 hours for slow cooker

Fancy Bean Substitutes: Scarlet Runner, Tepary, Good Mother Stallard

Indian Cauliflower Lentil Stew (Masoor Gobi Dal)

▶ SOY-FREE ▶ GLUTEN-FREE ▶ OIL-FREE OPTION*

Indian food is one of my favorites, and I can't ever have too much of it. Dal is a typical bean stew that has split lentils, but the variations are endless. This one adds cauliflower, which is always better with Indian spices! It's perfect served over rice.

1 to 2 tablespoon (15 to 28 ml) olive oil (*use water or broth)

½ small onion, minced

1 teaspoon mustard seeds

1 teaspoon coriander seeds

1 teaspoon cumin seeds

1 teaspoon garam masala

½ teaspoon turmeric

½ teaspoon chili powder

½ cup (96 g) moong dal (golden lentils)

½ cup (96 g) masoor dal (red lentils)

1 tablespoon (8 g) grated fresh ginger

2 cups (200 g) cauliflower florets

4 cups (950 ml) water

12 curry leaves, torn in half

1½ cups (270 g) diced tomatoes or 1 can (14.5 ounces, or 410 g)

Heat the olive oil over medium heat in a large soup pot. Add the onion and cook until translucent, about 5 minutes. Add all the spices and sauté a minute or two more until the spices become more fragrant.

Add the lentils, ginger, cauliflower, and water and cook for 20 to 30 minutes or until the lentils become soft.

Add the curry leaves and tomatoes and cook for 10 to 15 minutes more until the tomatoes break down. Serve over rice.

....

YIELD: 8 servings

PER 1-CUP SERVING (235 ML) (DOES NOT INCLUDE RICE): 64.9 calories; 1.9 g total fat; 0.3 g saturated fat; 3.3 g protein; 9.0 g carbohydrate; 3.2 g dietary fiber; 0 mg cholesterol.

TOTAL PREP TIME: 15 minutes

TOTAL COOKING TIME: 35 to 50 minutes

Pineapple Rum Beans over Coconut Lime Sweet Potatoes

▶ SOY-FREE ▶ GLUTEN-FREE ▶ OIL-FREE OPTION*

The beans are tasty by themselves but are transformed into something amazing once they're paired with the Coconut Lime Sweet Potatoes.

1 to 2 tablespoons (15 to 28 ml) olive oil (*use water or broth)

½ small onion, minced

2 cloves garlic, minced

1 cup (155 g) pineapple, chopped small

3 cups (513 g) cooked pinto or black beans or 2 cans (15 ounces, or 425 g each), rinsed and drained

2 tablespoons (28 ml) rum

1 teaspoon thyme

1 teaspoon smoked paprika

1 teaspoon marjoram

½ teaspoon ground cumin

¼ to ½ teaspoon salt (plain or smoked)

Black pepper, to taste

Cayenne pepper, to taste

Heat the oil in a medium saucepan over medium heat. Add the onion and sauté until translucent, about 5 minutes. Add the garlic and sauté for 1 minute more.

Add the pineapple, beans, rum, thyme, paprika, marjoram, and cumin. Cook over medium heat until it starts simmering and then decrease the heat to low and cover. Simmer for 25 to 35 minutes until the flavors meld. Season with salt, pepper, and cayenne.

YIELD: 4 servings

PER 1 CUP (235 ML) PINEAPPLE RUM BEANS: 270.6 calories; 7.6 g total fat; 1.1 g saturated fat; 11.8 g protein; 36.6 g carbohydrate; 11.9 g dietary fiber; 0 mg cholesterol.

TOTAL PREP TIME: 20 minutes

TOTAL COOKING TIME: 30 to 40 minutes

Coconut Lime Sweet Potatoes

▶ SOY-FREE ▶ GLUTEN-FREE ▶ OIL-FREE

4 medium sweet potatoes, baked or peeled and boiled

½ cup (120 ml) light coconut milk

Zest and juice of 1 large lime

Salt and pepper, to taste

If using baked sweet potatoes, cut in half and scrape the flesh into a saucepan (or just add if boiled). Mash the potatoes with the coconut milk and lime zest and juice until smooth. Taste, add salt and pepper, and taste again. You can add more lime juice or coconut milk if needed.

YIELD: 4 servings

PER 1½ CUPS (340 G): 123.0 calories; 2.1 g total fat; 1.6 g saturated fat; 2.7 g protein; 24.8 g carbohydrate; 3.8 g dietary fiber; 0 mg cholesterol.

TOTAL PREP TIME: 20 minutes

TOTAL COOKING TIME: 20 to 40 minutes

Ratatouille with White Beans

▶ SOY-FREE ▶ OIL-FREE OPTION* ▶ GLUTEN-FREE

This is the quintessential summer dish. Just one trip to the farmers' market will yield beautiful tomatoes, eggplants, summer squash, and fresh herbs. Switch up the colors of all the veggies to make it surprising. Try orange or yellow tomatoes, pattypan squash, and whatever odd-colored eggplant you find just for fun.

1 to 2 tablespoon (15 to 28 ml) olive oil (*use water or broth)

½ small onion, minced

2 cloves garlic, minced

3 cups (540 g) diced fresh tomatoes or 2 cans (14.5 ounces, or 410 g each)

½ medium eggplant, diced

1 medium summer squash, diced

1½ cups (358 g) cooked white beans or 1 can (15 ounces, or 425 g), rinsed and drained

4 (2 inch, or 5 cm) sprigs thyme or 2 teaspoons dried

4 (2 inch, or 5 cm) sprigs oregano or 1 teaspoon dried

1 teaspoon dried basil or 2 tablespoons (5 g) chopped fresh

Salt and pepper, to taste

Heat the olive oil over medium heat in a medium soup pot. Add the onion and cook until translucent, about 5 minutes. Add the garlic and sauté a minute more.

Add the tomatoes, eggplant, squash, beans, thyme, oregano, and dried basil (if using fresh add it at the end). Cover and cook for 30 to 45 minutes or until the tomatoes have broken down and the eggplant is soft. Remove the herb stems. If you are using fresh basil, add it in right before serving and then add salt and pepper to taste.

Serving Suggestions & Variations

Serve leftovers cold, spread over whole-grain toast. Everyone loves bruschetta, and this is a perfect topping for dinner on the hottest day of the year. (It's also good as a cold salad in a pinch.)

Fancy Bean Substitutes: Flageolet, European Solider, Vallarta, Alubia Blanca

YIELD: 4 servings

PER 2-CUP (475 ML) SERVING: 192.4 calories; 7.4 g total fat; 1.0 g saturated fat; 7.8 g protein; 26.4 g carbohydrate; 6.8 g dietary fiber; 0 mg cholesterol.

TOTAL PREP TIME: 20 minutes

TOTAL COOKING TIME: 35 to 50 minutes

Solstice Beans with Pumpkin and Greens

▶ SOY-FREE ▶ OIL-FREE OPTION* ▶ GLUTEN-FREE

No one will suspect there is pumpkin in this because the pumpkin actually breaks down and makes a nice sauce. Also, by chopping the greens small, you cut down on cooking time and might be able to tempt your picky eater into trying this wonderful winter stew.

3 cups (513 g) cooked pinto beans or 2 cans (15 ounces, or 425 g each), rinsed and drained

3 cups (348 g) peeled and cubed pumpkin

1 cup (235 ml) water

1 veggie bouillon cube

1 teaspoon jerk seasoning

1 tablespoon (15 ml) red or port wine

Red pepper flakes or cayenne pepper, to taste

2 cups (134 g) chopped kale or other greens, stems removed

Salt and pepper, to taste

∴∴∴∴∴∴∴∴∴∴∴∴∴∴∴∴∴∴∴∴∴∴∴∴∴∴

YIELD: 4 servings

PER 2-CUP (475 ML) SERVING: 221.6 calories; 0.8 g total fat; 0.2 g saturated fat; 11.4 g protein; 44.1 g carbohydrate; 12.6 g dietary fiber; 0 mg cholesterol.

TOTAL PREP TIME: 20 minutes

TOTAL COOKING TIME: 30 to 40 minutes for stove top, 6 to 8 hours for slow cooker

STOVE-TOP DIRECTIONS*

To a large soup pot, add the pinto beans, pumpkin, water, bouillon, jerk seasoning, wine, and red pepper flakes. Cook, covered, over medium heat until the pumpkin begins to break down and it almost looks like it was never there. Add more water as needed during this time. It should take about 20 to 30 minutes.

Once the pumpkin is cooked down, add the kale and cook, uncovered, until the kale turns bright green or is cooked as you like it. Taste and add salt and pepper. Also adjust the hot pepper or jerk seasoning if needed.

Serve over cornbread for a hearty winter meal.

SLOW COOKER DIRECTIONS

Add the pinto beans, pumpkin, water, bouillon, jerk seasoning, wine, and red pepper flakes to an oiled crock. Cook on low for 6 to 8 hours.

Thirty minutes before serving: If there are any chunks of pumpkin that haven't melted into the stew, mash them with a fork. Add the kale and cook until tender, about 40 minutes. Add salt and pepper to taste and add more pepper or jerk seasoning if needed.

Fancy Bean Substitutes: Rio Zape, Goat's Eye, Cranberry

Refried Bolita or Pinto Beans

▶ SOY-FREE ▶ GLUTEN-FREE ▶ OIL-FREE OPTION*

This recipe is low-fat with only a tablespoon (15 ml) of olive oil for the whole batch, but you can sauté the veggies in water to make it completely fat-free. On the other hand, this dish mixed with a shredded vegan Mexican cheese makes a great bean-dip dinner.

1 to 2 tablespoons (15 to 28 ml) olive oil (*use water or broth)

½ small onion, minced

2 cloves garlic, minced

½ bell pepper, cored, seeded, and minced

1 teaspoon cumin

½ to 2 teaspoons chili powder

A few drops liquid smoke (optional)

3 cups (513 g) cooked bolita or pinto beans or 2 cans (15 ounces, or 425 g each), rinsed and drained

Heat a large sauté pan over medium heat. Add the onion and cook until translucent, about 5 minutes. Then add the garlic, bell pepper, cumin, chili powder, and liquid smoke and sauté a minute or two more.

Add the beans and if they are a bit dry, add water as needed. Stir and mash the beans so they are no longer whole. You can make them as smooth or chunky as you like. I like mine smooth. Add water as many times as you need to during the process.

YIELD: 6 servings

PER ½-CUP (120 ML) SERVING: 107.7 calories; 4.5 g total fat; 0.6 g saturated fat; 5.0 g protein; 15.1 g carbohydrate; 3.6 g dietary fiber; 0 mg cholesterol.

TOTAL PREP TIME: 20 minutes

TOTAL COOKING TIME: 10 to 15 minutes

Serving Suggestions & Variations

Add ½ to 1 cup (56 to 112 g) shredded vegan cheese; Pepper Jack or Mexican works great!

Fancy Bean Substitutes: Rio Zape, Goat's Eye, Cranberry

Margarita Chili Beans

▶ SOY-FREE ▶ GLUTEN-FREE ▶ OIL-FREE OPTION*

These beans go perfectly with a margarita or a sparkling lime mocktail. The tequila cooks down to make a rich broth. Coconut-lime smoked salt can be found through the Resources Guide, page 185.

2 tablespoons (28 ml) olive oil (*use water or broth)

½ small onion, minced

3 cloves garlic, minced

1 jalapeño, seeded and minced

½ to 1 cup (120 ml to 235 ml) water

¼ cup (60 ml) tequila

3 cups (513 g) cooked pinto beans or 2 cans (15 ounces, or 425 g each), rinsed and drained

½ teaspoon ground rosemary

¼ teaspoon ground cumin

¼ teaspoon ancho chile powder (or your favorite chili powder)

Juice and zest of 1 lime

Salt, to taste

Coconut-lime smoked salt, for garnish (optional)

::

YIELD: 4 servings

PER 1-CUP (235 ML) SERVING: 280.8 calories; 7.5 g total fat; 1.1 g saturated fat; 11.0 g protein; 36.2 g carbohydrate; 11.5 g dietary fiber; 0 mg cholesterol.

TOTAL PREP TIME: 15 minutes

TOTAL COOKING TIME: 35 to 50 minutes for stove top, 7 to 9 hours for slow cooker

STOVE-TOP DIRECTIONS

Heat the oil in a large saucepan over medium heat. Add the onion and sauté until translucent, about 5 minutes. Then add the garlic and sauté for 2 minutes more.

Add the jalapeño, ½ cup (120 ml) of the water, tequila, beans, rosemary, cumin, chili powder, and lime juice and zest. Cook over low heat, covered, for 30 to 45 minutes, or until the flavors have come together. Add some or all of the remaining ½ cup (120 ml) water during cooking if the stew starts to dry out. Season with salt.

If you have some coconut-lime salt, sprinkle that on top just before serving to wow all your guests.

SLOW COOKER DIRECTIONS

Heat the oil in a 2-quart (1.8 L) sauté pan over medium heat. Add the onion and sauté until translucent, about 5 minutes. Add the garlic and sauté for 2 minutes more.

Add everything except for the lime juice and lime zest to a 4-quart (3.6-L) slow cooker. Cook on low for 7 to 9 hours. About 30 minutes before serving, add the lime zest and juice, taste, and add salt.

Did You Know?

You can make your own coconut-lime salt if you can't find any near you. Add about 2 tablespoons (11 g) dried coconut to a food processor and process until it's almost a powder. Add the zest of 1 lime and 2 to 4 tablespoons salt (to taste) and process again. Store in a tightly lidded container.

Kalpana's Black-Eyed Pea Curry ▸

▸ SOY-FREE ▸ GLUTEN-FREE

Kalpana's black-eyed peas are too good not to be shared.

1 to 2 tablespoons (15 to 28 ml) olive oil

1 medium red onion, diced

1 teaspoon cumin seeds

½ teaspoon turmeric

1 teaspoon ground coriander

1½ cups (270 g) diced fresh tomatoes

Salt, to taste

3 cups (750 g) cooked black-eyed peas or 2 cans (15 ounces, or 420 g each), rinsed and drained

Juice of ½ lime

½ teaspoon garam masala

Pinch of asafoetida (optional)

¼ to ½ teaspoon red chili powder

½ cup (8 g) chopped fresh cilantro

Heat the oil in a large sauté pan over medium heat. Add the onion and cumin seeds and cook until the onion is just beginning to brown and the cumin seeds have become fragrant, about 5 minutes.

Add the turmeric, coriander, and tomatoes with a pinch of salt. Cook until the tomatoes start breaking down, 10 to 15 minutes.

Add the peas, lime juice, garam masala, asafoetida, chili powder, and fresh cilantro. Cook over medium-low heat until heated through, 5 to 10 minutes.

YIELD: 4 servings

PER 1-CUP (225 G) SERVING: 209.9 calories; 7.7 g total fat; 0.9 g saturated fat; 5.0 g protein; 32.3 g carbohydrate; 8.1 g dietary fiber; 0 mg cholesterol.

TOTAL PREP TIME: 15 minutes

TOTAL COOKING TIME: 20 to 30 minutes

Green Beans Poriyal ▸

▸ SOY-FREE ▸ GLUTEN-FREE

Kalpana's dry green bean curry with coconut.

1 teaspoon urad dal (split skinned black lentils)

1 teaspoon channa dal (split skinned chickpeas)

1 to 2 tablespoons (15 to 28 ml) olive oil

1 teaspoon mustard seeds

Pinch of asafoetida (optional)

12 curry leaves, fresh or dried, torn in half

½ teaspoon turmeric

½ green chile, seeded and minced

2 pounds (910 g) green string beans, cut small

½ teaspoon salt, or to taste

¼ cup (60 ml) water

3 to 4 tablespoons (16 to 21 g) finely shredded dried coconut

¼ cup (4 g) chopped fresh cilantro

Rinse and soak the urad dal and channa dal in a bowl with water to cover for at least 5 minutes. Drain.

Heat the oil in a large sauté pan over medium heat. Add the mustard seeds, asafoetida, curry leaves, and dals and sauté until the dals turn a light brown. Add the turmeric, chile, green beans, salt, and water and cook, covered, over medium-low heat. Stir every few minutes and add more water, if needed. Cook until the green beans are tender but not mushy. Mix in the coconut and cilantro.

YIELD: 4 servings

PER ½-CUP (115 G) SERVING: 122.4 calories; 11.1 g total fat; 3.4 g saturated fat; 1.5 g protein; 7.1 g carbohydrate; 2.0 g dietary fiber; 0 mg cholesterol.

TOTAL PREP TIME: 15 minutes

TOTAL COOKING TIME: 10 to 15 minutes

Apple Baked Beans

▶ SOY-FREE ▶ GLUTEN-FREE ▶ OIL-FREE

I lived most of my life not realizing there was a great baked bean debate. I always thought baked beans were made from white beans, but there are those who favor pintos and even others who stray into the unknown, like I do. I like to use a combo fancy bean substitution of Rio Zape and yellow-eyed peas, but you can use the ones you grew up with, or make your own mark on the baked bean scene.

1½ cups (257 g) cooked pinto or white beans (Northern or navy) or 1 can (15 ounces, or 425 g), rinsed and drained

2 apples, peeled and minced

1 can (14.5 ounces, or 410 g) crushed tomatoes or diced tomatoes processed into a purèe

4 teaspoons (20 g) Dijon mustard

2 tablespoons (40 g) molasses

1 to 2 tablespoons (15 to 28 ml) apple cider vinegar

½ teaspoon smoked paprika

½ cup (120 ml) water

1 (2 inch, or 5 cm) sprig fresh rosemary or ½ teaspoon ground dried

4 (2 inch, or 5 cm) sprigs fresh thyme or 1 teaspoon dried

A few drops liquid smoke (optional)

¼ to ½ teaspoon salt

Black pepper, to taste

....

YIELD: 4 servings

PER 1½-CUP (355 ML) SERVING: 148.0 calories; 1.4 g total fat; 0.1 g saturated fat; 5.8 g protein; 33.1 g carbohydrate; 8.6 g dietary fiber; 0 mg cholesterol.

TOTAL PREP TIME: 20 minutes

TOTAL COOKING TIME: 60 to 90 minutes for stove top, 7 to 9 hours for slow cooker

STOVE-TOP DIRECTIONS

Combine everything except the salt and pepper in a saucepan and cook over medium heat until it begins to simmer. Then cover and cook on low until the beans are tender, about 1½ hours. (Note that the time will change depending on the type, size, and age of the beans you pick.)

When the beans are tender, add salt and pepper to make it just the way you like it.

SLOW COOKER DIRECTIONS

Combine everything except the salt and pepper in a 4-quart (3.8 L) slow cooker and cook on low for 7 to 9 hours. Taste, add salt and pepper, and then taste again. Adjust if needed.

Did You Know?

Rio Zape is a great bean to use in any recipes that call for pinto beans. They cook down like pintos but are slightly denser. These are also known as Hopi string beans.

Fancy Bean Substitutes: Flageolet, European Solider, Vallarta, Alubia Blanca, Rio Zape, Yellow-Eyed Peas, Goat's Eye, Cranberry

Cheezy Yellow-Eyed Peas

▶ SOY-FREE OPTION* ▶ GLUTEN-FREE ▶ OIL-FREE

These comforting beans make their own tasty gravy. Serve over piping hot corn-bread to sop up all the goodness. Feel free to use black-eyed peas if you don't have yellow-eyed ones.

2 cups (475 ml) water

3 cups (495 g) cooked yellow-eyed peas or 2 cans (15 ounces, or 425 g) black-eyed peas, rinsed and drained

2 small carrots, minced (peeled if not organic)

2 small parsnips, peeled and minced

1 medium turnip, peeled and minced

2 (2 inch, or 5 cm) sprigs fresh rosemary or 1 teaspoon ground dried

¼ to ½ cup (24 to 48 g) nutritional yeast

¼ cup (60 ml) nondairy milk (*use soy-free)

Salt and pepper, to taste

Jalapeño salt, for topping (optional)

Cornbread, for serving

:::

YIELD: 4 servings

PER 1½-CUP (355 ML) SERVING (DOES NOT INCLUDE CORNBREAD): 88.2 calories; 0.6 g total fat; 0 g saturated fat; 3.4 g protein; 18.3 g carbohydrate; 4.7 g dietary fiber; 0 mg cholesterol.

TOTAL PREP TIME: 20 minutes

TOTAL COOKING TIME: 15 to 25 minutes for stove top, 6 to 9 hours for slow cooker

STOVE-TOP DIRECTIONS

Add the water, beans, carrots, parsnips, turnip, and rosemary to a medium saucepan and cook, covered, over medium heat until the mixture thickens and beans begin to break down, about 15 to 25 minutes. (You can mash a few of the beans if they aren't getting as creamy as you want them.)

Before serving, add ¼ cup (24 g) of the nutritional yeast and the milk, mix, and taste. Add salt, pepper, jalapeño salt, and some or all of the remaining ¼ cup (24 g) nutritional yeast if you'd like. Serve with cornbread.

SLOW COOKER DIRECTIONS

Add the water, beans, carrots, parsnips, turnip, and rosemary to a slow cooker and cook on low for 6 to 9 hours.

Before serving, add ¼ cup (24 g) of the nutritional yeast and the milk, mix, and taste. Add salt, pepper, jalapeño salt, and some or all of the remaining ¼ cup (24 g) nutritional yeast if you'd like. Serve with cornbread.

Vaquero Bean Tempeh Chili

▶ GLUTEN-FREE ▶ OIL-FREE OPTION* ▶ SOY-FREE OPTION**

This chili has a very rich, dark flavor from the combination of chiles. If you decide to buy heirloom beans from Rancho Gordo (see Resources Guide, page 185), be sure to order some of their yummy chili powders.

2 tablespoons (28 ml) olive oil (*use water or broth)

½ small onion, minced

3 cloves garlic, minced

8 ounces (225 g) soy tempeh, diced (**use seitan)

6 cups (1.5 kg) cooked Vaquero beans or 3 cans (15 ounces, or 425 g each) pinto or black beans, rinsed and drained

1 cup (235 ml) water

1 can (14.5 ounces, or 410 g) diced tomatoes or 1½ cups (270 g) chopped fresh

1 tablespoon (16 g) tomato paste

1 teaspoon chili powder

1 teaspoon pasilla chile powder

1 teaspoon oregano

½ teaspoon paprika

¼ to ½ teaspoon chipotle powder

Salt (smoked or plain), to taste

Vegan sour cream **or Cashew Cream (page 28), for serving

Heat the olive oil in a large saucepan over medium heat. Add the onion and sauté until translucent, about 5 minutes. Then add the garlic and sauté for a few more minutes.

Add everything else except the salt and sour cream. Cook over medium heat and turn to low as soon as it starts to simmer. Cover and cook for 30 to 40 minutes until piping hot. Taste and season with salt. Serve topped with vegan sour cream.

Fancy Bean Substitutes: Black Calypso, Purple Runner, Goat's Eye

....

YIELD: 6 servings

PER 1½-CUP (355 ML) SERVING (DOES NOT INCLUDE VEGAN SOUR CREAM): 347.3 calories; 8.4 g total fat; 1.4 g saturated fat; 20.0 g protein; 51.0 g carbohydrate; 15.9 g dietary fiber; 0 mg cholesterol.

TOTAL PREP TIME: 20 minutes

TOTAL COOKING TIME: 40 to 50 minutes

Creole White Beans

▶ SOY-FREE ▶ GLUTEN-FREE ▶ OIL-FREE OPTION*

These are similar to the familiar red beans and rice, but aren't known as much outside of Louisiana. I like them because of the extra creaminess the white beans lend to the dish.

2 tablespoons (28 ml) olive oil (*use water or broth)

½ small onion, minced

1 bell pepper, cored, seeded, and minced

3 cloves garlic, minced

2 stalks celery, minced

1½ teaspoons thyme

1½ teaspoons smoked paprika

1 teaspoon oregano

¼ to ½ teaspoon cayenne pepper

2 bay leaves

2 tablespoons (12 g) veggie bouillon

1 cup (215 g) dried white beans plus 4 cups (950 ml) water or 2 cans (15 ounces, or 425 g each), rinsed and drained, plus 2 cups (475 ml) water

Salt and pepper, to taste

Cooked rice, for serving

::

YIELD: 4 servings

PER 1-CUP (235 ML) SERVING (DOES NOT INCLUDE RICE): 151.8 calories; 1.1 g total fat; 0.3 g saturated fat; 14.4 g protein; 21.0 g carbohydrate; 3.8 g dietary fiber; 0 mg cholesterol.

TOTAL PREP TIME: 20 minutes

TOTAL COOKING TIME: 30 to 90 minutes for stove top, 8 to 10 hours for slow cooker

STOVE-TOP DIRECTIONS

Heat the olive oil over medium heat in a soup pot. Add the onion and sauté until translucent, about 5 minutes, and then add the bell pepper and garlic. Sauté for 2 minutes more, and then add the celery, herbs, spices, bouillon, and dry or canned beans and appropriate amount of water.

Bring to a boil over high heat and then decrease the heat to low and cover. Cook until the beans are soft and ready to eat. It will only take about 15 to 20 minutes if you are using canned beans, but it will take 40 to 60 minutes for dried beans. If they are a little watery, increase the heat, uncover, and cook until they are the thickness you prefer. Remove the bay leaves. Taste and add salt and pepper to your liking. Serve over rice.

SLOW COOKER DIRECTIONS

Heat the olive oil over medium heat in a soup pot. Add the onion and sauté until translucent, about 5 minutes, and then add the bell pepper and garlic. Sauté for 2 minutes more. Transfer to the slow cooker and add the rest of the ingredients except the salt and pepper, but use only 3 cups (700 ml) water. Cook on low for 8 to 10 hours.

Remove the bay leaves. Taste and add salt and pepper to your liking. Serve over rice.

Fancy Bean Substitutes: Flageolet, European Solider, Vallarta, Alubia Blanca, or any other white bean

Hard Cider–Sauced Beans

▶ SOY-FREE ▶ GLUTEN-FREE OPTION* ▶ OIL-FREE

Serve these beans with a side of veggies and some crusty bread to make a complete dinner.

3 cups (513 g) cooked pinto beans or 2 cans (15 ounces, or 425 g each), rinsed and drained

1 bottle (12 ounces, or 355 ml) hard cider (*use gluten-free) or plain apple cider

½ small onion, minced

1 tablespoon (20 g) agave nectar

1 tablespoon (11 g) mustard

½ teaspoon liquid smoke

Salt and pepper, to taste

Add everything to a medium pot and heat over medium heat, covered, for 20 to 30 minutes until the hard cider reduces. If the sauce is still a little thin, smash a few of the beans and mix in to thicken the broth.

Fancy Bean Substitutes: Rio Zape, Goat's Eye, Cranberry

YIELD: 4 servings

PER 1-CUP (235 ML) SERVING: 159.2 calories; 0 g total fat; 0 g saturated fat; 7.0 g protein; 28.3 g carbohydrate; 8.1 g dietary fiber; 0 mg cholesterol.

TOTAL PREP TIME: 10 minutes

TOTAL COOKING TIME: 20 to 30 minutes

Baked Lima Beans in Tomato Sauce

▶ SOY-FREE ▶ GLUTEN-FREE ▶ OIL-FREE OPTION*

These dried lima beans are cooked up in an herbed tomato broth right in your oven. It takes about an hour, but you don't have to babysit this perfect winter dinner.

1 can (28 ounces, or 785 g) crushed tomatoes (with basil if possible)

1 teaspoon dried oregano

1 teaspoon dried basil

½ teaspoon marjoram

2 cups (296 g) dried lima beans

½ small onion, chopped

½ bell pepper, cored, seeded, and chopped

Chopped parsley, for garnish

:::

YIELD: 6 servings

PER 1-CUP (235 ML) SERVING: 200 calories; 0 g total fat; 0 g saturated fat; 14.3 g protein; 43.1 g carbohydrate; 13.0 g dietary fiber; 0 mg cholesterol.

TOTAL PREP TIME: 10 minutes

TOTAL COOKING TIME: 45 to 60 minutes

Preheat the oven to 350°F (180°C, or gas mark 4). Oil a rectangular casserole pan *or use a nonstick pan.

Put the tomatoes, oregano, basil, and marjoram into a food processor and purée. Pour into the pan and add the lima beans, onion, and pepper. (This is one time I do not pre-sauté the onion. It cooks enough in the sauce.)

Mix well and then cover with foil or an oven-safe lid and cook for 45 to 60 minutes or until the lima beans are completely cooked through but not mushy. Check every 20 minutes and stir.

Did You Know?

In the summer you can purée those extra bits of herbs with some olive oil or water and freeze them in ice-cube trays. This is the best (and cheapest) way to enjoy fresh herbs when they are not in season.

Fancy Bean Substitutes: Any of the runner beans (scarlet, purple, black, etc.) would be great in this dish.

Down-Home Greens and Beans Sautè

▶ SOY-FREE ▶ GLUTEN-FREE ▶ OIL-FREE OPTION*

When the beautiful greens show up at the market, this is the quick dinner to use them in. The longest part of this recipe is prepping the greens, and you can always do that the night before. This works especially well with collards after the first frost in the fall. That's when they lose their bitterness and taste amazing.

1 to 2 tablespoons (15 to 28 ml) olive oil (*use water or broth)

½ small onion, minced

2 cloves garlic, minced

2 medium carrots, thinly sliced (peeled if not organic), or 1 small sweet potato, peeled and diced

2 vegetable bouillon cubes

½ teaspoon liquid smoke

2 cups (475 ml) water

8 cups (288 g) greens, stems removed and torn into small pieces

1½ cups (257 g) cooked pinto beans or 1 can (15 ounces, or 425 g), rinsed and drained

Hot sauce, for serving (optional)

:::

YIELD: 4 servings

PER 1-CUP (255 G) SERVING: 165.2 calories; 7.2 g total fat; 1.0 g saturated fat; 6.8 g protein; 23.8 g carbohydrate; 9.0 g dietary fiber; 0 mg cholesterol.

TOTAL PREP TIME: 15 minutes

TOTAL COOKING TIME: 25 to 30 minutes

Heat the oil in a large sauté pan over medium heat. Add onion and cook until translucent, about 5 minutes. Add the garlic and carrots and sauté another minute or two more. Add the bouillon, liquid smoke, and water, then turn the heat up to medium-high, and cook until the carrots are tender, about 10 minutes.

Add the greens a few handfuls at a time to the pan. This will allow them to reduce in volume so you can fit them all. Add more water if the pan gets too dry, but at the end you don't want much liquid, so be stingier near the end of cooking time.

Once all the greens are in the pan, add the beans and cook until the beans are heated through and the greens are tender but still a vibrant green color, 5 to 10 minutes.

Serve with a side of rice or cornbread and top with your favorite hot sauce.

Fancy Bean Substitutes: Rio Zape, Goat's Eye, Cranberry

Good Mother Stallard Beans

▶ SOY-FREE ▶ GLUTEN-FREE ▶ OIL-FREE

This is a simple recipe, but unlike most of the recipes in this book, it does not use precooked beans. The best part of this is the beautiful broth, called pot liquor, that the beans make as they cook. This is my favorite way to feature many heirloom beans, but especially Good Mother Stallard beans.

2 cups (430 g) dried Good Mother Stallard beans, rinsed and picked through (see page 8)

6 cups (1.4 L) water

2 bay leaves

1 (2 inch, or 5 cm) sprig fresh rosemary

2 carrots, diced (peeled if not organic)

Salt and pepper, to taste

YIELD: 6 servings

PER 1-CUP (235 ML) SERVING: 95.8 calories; 0.4 g total fat; 0.1 g saturated fat; 5.1 g protein; 18.7 g carbohydrate; 6.1 g dietary fiber; 0 mg cholesterol.

TOTAL PREP TIME: 20 minutes

TOTAL COOKING TIME: 2 to 3 hours for stove top, 7 to 10 hours for slow cooker

STOVE-TOP DIRECTIONS

Add everything except the salt and pepper to a soup pot. Bring to a boil, cover, and decrease the heat to medium-low. Cook until the beans are tender, 2 to 3 hours. If your beans are older, it can take as much as twice as long.

Add salt and pepper, remove the bay leaves and herb sprig, and then dig into a bowl of home-cooked goodness!

SLOW COOKER DIRECTIONS

Add everything except the salt and pepper to the slow cooker and cook on low for 7 to 10 hours. When finished, add salt and pepper and remove the bay leaves and herb sprig.

Serving Suggestions & Variations

Soak the beans during the day while you're at work to cut the cooking time in half.

Fancy Bean Substitutes: Goat's Eye, Cranberry

Did You Know?

Good Mother Stallard beans have a thick skin similar to that of kidney beans but more with swollen centers and are almost like tiny, rounded footballs. They produce a broth that's amazing, so resist the urge to fancy them up—just enjoy their natural flavors.

Black-Eyed Peas with Grit Cakes

▶ SOY-FREE OPTION* ▶ GLUTEN-FREE ▶ OIL-FREE OPTION**

Creamy beans rest on top of grit cakes to make a delicious Southern-style meal. If you can find some jalapeño salt, it really adds a special touch to this dish.

FOR THE BEANS

1 pound (455 g) dried black-eyed peas

3 cloves garlic, minced

3 bay leaves

6 cups (1.4 L) water, or enough to cover the beans and about 1 inch (2.5 cm) above

1 to 2 teaspoons Cajun Spice Blend (page 29)

A few drops of liquid smoke

Chipotle powder or other hot chile powder, to taste

Smoked salt, jalapeño salt, and pepper, to taste

Hot sauce, for serving

FOR THE GRIT CAKES

2 cups (475 ml) unsweetened nondairy milk (*use soy-free)

2 cups (475 ml) water

1 veggie bouillon cube

1 cup (140 g) regular grits (not instant or quick cooking!)

Salt and pepper, to taste

:::

YIELD: 6 servings

PER 1-CUP (235 ML) SERVING OF BEANS: 162.2 calories; 1.0 g total fat; 0 g saturated fat; 5.1 g protein; 34.5 g carbohydrate; 8.0 g dietary fiber; 0 mg cholesterol.

PER ⅙ PIECE OF GRIT CAKE: 44.0 calories; 1.0 g total fat; 0 g saturated fat; 0.9 g protein; 7.4 g carbohydrate; 0.6 g dietary fiber; 0 mg cholesterol.

TOTAL PREP TIME: 20 minutes

TOTAL COOKING TIME: 1½ to 2 hours for stove top, 7 to 9 hours for slow cooker

STOVE-TOP DIRECTIONS

To make the beans, add everything except the salts and hot sauce to a medium soup pot. Bring to a boil and then decrease the heat to medium-low and cover. Cook until the black-eyed peas are tender, about 1 to 1½ hours. Remove the bay leaves. Taste and add smoked salt, pepper, and jalapeño salt.

To make the grit cakes, preheat the oven to 350°F (180°C, or gas mark 4) and oil a sheet pan **or line with parchment paper.

Add the nondairy milk, water, and bouillon to a heavy saucepan. Bring almost to a boil and then decrease the heat to a simmer. Now add the grits. Stir every five minutes or the bottom of the pan will burn. Cook for 30 to 40 minutes or until you taste them and they aren't hard. They won't get as soft as some grains, but you will be able to tell the difference.

Remove the grits from the heat and spread on the prepared sheet pan. They will start to solidify quickly. Bake in the oven for about 15 minutes or until the middle is hot. Cut into squares and serve with the beans on top. Pass the hot sauce at the table.

SLOW COOKER DIRECTIONS (FOR THE PEAS)

To make the beans, add everything except the salts and hot sauce to your slow cooker. Cook on low for 7 to 9 hours. Right before serving, taste and adjust the seasonings if needed and add salt and pepper. Remove the bay leaves.

Prepare the grit cakes and serve as above.

Fancy Bean Substitute: Yellow-Eyed Peas

Tomato Rosemary White Beans

▶ SOY-FREE ▶ GLUTEN-FREE ▶ OIL-FREE

This simple bean dish is perfect over toasted bread, rice, or a bed of creamy polenta. It's easy to make but really dresses up dinner.

3 cups (537 g) cooked white beans or 2 cans (15 ounces, or 425 g each), rinsed and drained

2 cloves garlic, minced

1-inch (2.5 cm) strip lemon zest

1½ cups (270 g) diced fresh tomatoes or 1 can (14.5 ounces, or 410 g)

2 (1 inch, or 2.5 cm) sprigs fresh thyme or 1 teaspoon dried

2 (1 inch, or 2.5 cm) sprigs fresh rosemary or 1 teaspoon dried or ½ teaspoon ground

Salt and pepper, to taste

....

YIELD: 4 servings

PER 1-CUP (235 ML) SERVING: 257.7 calories; 0.6 g total fat; 0.1 g saturated fat; 14.4 g protein; 48.8 g carbohydrate; 9.5 g dietary fiber; 0 mg cholesterol.

TOTAL PREP TIME: 15 minutes

TOTAL COOKING TIME: 30 to 45 minutes for stove top, 8 to 9 hours for slow cooker

STOVE-TOP DIRECTIONS

Add everything except the salt and pepper to a soup pot and cook on low for 30 to 45 minutes until the flavors meld. Taste and then season with salt and pepper.

SLOW COOKER DIRECTIONS

Add everything except the salt and pepper to a 4-quart (3.8 L) slow cooker and cook on low for 8 to 9 hours. Taste and then season with salt and pepper.

Fancy Bean Substitutes: Flageolet, European Solider, Vallarta, Alubia Blanca

Beluga Lentil Stew over Fresh Spinach

▶ SOY-FREE ▶ GLUTEN-FREE ▶ OIL-FREE OPTION*

Rosemary-scented shiny black lentils over bright green spinach with orange flecks of carrot are here to brighten up your night.

2 tablespoons (28 ml) olive oil (*use water or broth)

½ small onion, minced

2 cloves garlic, minced

1 cup (192 g) beluga lentils (or regular brown lentils)

4 cups (945 ml) water

2 cubes vegetable bouillon

½ cup (65 g) diced carrot (peeled if not organic)

1 stalk celery, diced

1 sprig fresh rosemary

¼ to ½ teaspoon liquid smoke

Salt and pepper, to taste

4 cups (120 g) baby spinach, for serving

Balsamic vinegar, for drizzling (I use juniper berry balsamic)

:::

YIELD: 3 servings

PER SERVING: 153.7 calories; 5.0 g total fat; 0.7 g saturated fat; 8.4 g protein; 20.3 g carbohydrate; 7.2 g dietary fiber; 0 mg cholesterol.

TOTAL PREP TIME: 20 minutes

TOTAL COOKING TIME: 25 to 35 minutes

Heat the oil in a medium-size pot. Add the onion and cook until translucent, about 5 minutes. Then add the garlic and cook for 1 minute more. Add the lentils, water, bouillon, carrot, celery, rosemary, and liquid smoke.

Turn the heat to high and bring to a boil. After boiling for about a minute, turn it down to a simmer. Cook for 20 to 30 minutes or until the lentils are tender. If there is still too much liquid for your liking, turn the heat up to medium-high and cook until they are the way you like them. Conversely, feel free to add more water if they get too thick during cooking.

Remove from the heat and add salt and pepper to taste. Ladle over about 1 ⅓ cups (40 g) fresh baby spinach and drizzle each serving with balsamic vinegar. This will lightly cook the spinach.

Serving Suggestions & Variations

Add a seared plank of tofu or tempeh or a Baked Crispy Chickpea Seitan Patty (page 22) on top.

8

CASSEROLES, PASTAS, AND MORE

One-Dish Meals

One-dish meals are perfect for weeknight dinners. You can even assemble recipes like the Chock-Full of Veggies Pot Pie and Eggplant Lasagna the day before and just do the cooking once you get home from work. If you didn't plan ahead, the Stove-Top Mac 'n Beany comes together quickly and you can feel good feeding it to your family. There are one-dish bean and grain dishes for you to try out as well, so you can spend a month or two just on this chapter.

Inside-Out Enchilada Casserole

▶ SOY-FREE OPTION* ▶ OIL-FREE OPTION** ▶ GLUTEN-FREE

These enchiladas wear their cheeziness on the outside and have all the flavors of a typical enchilada sauce on the inside. Change up the veggies on the inside depending on the season or what you have on hand.

2 tablespoons (28 ml) olive oil (**use water or broth)

½ small onion, minced

3 cloves garlic, minced

1 teaspoon ground cumin

1 teaspoon chili powder

1 teaspoon smoked paprika

1½ cups (270 g) diced fresh tomatoes or 1 can (14.5 ounces, or 410 g)

Salt and pepper, to taste

1 can (15 ounces, or 425 g) pinto beans, drained and rinsed, or 1½ cups (340 g) chopped veggies

1 can (15 ounces, or 425 g) black beans, drained and rinsed, or 1½ cups (340 g) chopped veggies

1½ cups (180 g) diced summer squash

12 (6 inch, or 15 cm) corn tortillas

1 recipe Vegan Cashew-Bean Queso (page 58) mixed with ½ to 1 cup (120 to 235 ml) nondairy milk to make it pourable (*use soy-free)

YIELD: 12 enchiladas

PER ENCHILADA: 186.8 calories; 3.8 g total fat; 0.5 g saturated fat; 8.2 g protein; 31.6 g carbohydrate; 8.4 g dietary fiber; 0 mg cholesterol.

TOTAL PREP TIME: 15 minutes

TOTAL COOKING TIME: 45 to 60 minutes

Preheat the oven to 350°F (180°C, or gas mark 4). Oil an 11 x 8-inch (28 x 20 cm) casserole pan.

Heat the oil in a large sauté pan over medium heat and cook the onion until translucent, about 5 minutes. Add the garlic and spices and sauté 1 minute more.

Add the tomatoes and cook for 15 to 20 minutes.

Transfer the tomato mixture to a food processor and process until smooth. Add salt and pepper to taste.

In a large bowl, combine the tomato mixture, beans, and summer squash. This will be the filling for the tortillas.

Soften the tortillas by placing in a microwave for 15 seconds covered by a damp paper towel or by heating them in a warm sauté pan. This will help them stay together better when you roll them. Hate this step? Just layer tortillas under and over the filling instead of rolling them up.

Spread a thin layer of queso on the bottom of the prepared pan. Take each tortilla and add a few tablespoons (45 to 55 g) of filling, roll, and place seam side down in the pan. Repeat until the pan is full and all tortillas have been used. If you have some extra filling, just sprinkle it over the top of the tortillas.

Spread the rest of the queso over the top, cover with foil, and bake until heated all the way through, about 30 to 45 minutes.

Fancy Bean Substitutes: Rio Zape, Goat's Eye, Cranberry, Black Calypso, Vaquero

White Bean Potato Tart

▶ GLUTEN-FREE OPTION* ▶ SOY-FREE OPTION** ▶ OIL-FREE OPTION***

This tart looks impressive when made in a proper fluted tart pan. It does take a bit of work to get the crust in all the nooks and crannies, but it's worth it to hear the ooohs and ahhs.

FOR THE CRUST

1½ cups (180 g) whole wheat pastry flour (*use gluten-free)

¾ cup (180 g) unsweetened vegan yogurt (**use plain coconut yogurt)

2 tablespoons (12 g) nutritional yeast

¼ teaspoon salt

FOR THE FILLING

1½ cups (358 g) cooked white beans or 1 can (15 ounces, or 425 g), rinsed and drained

½ cup (120 ml) unsweetened nondairy milk (**use soy-free)

¼ cup (24 g) nutritional yeast

A few drops of liquid smoke (optional)

Salt and pepper, to taste

2 large potatoes or equivalent baby potatoes, boiled until just tender, then sliced (peel if not organic)

Smoked paprika, for topping

Smoked salt, for topping

Shredded vegan cheese (**omit)

:::

YIELD: 8 servings

PER SERVING (DOES NOT INCLUDE VEGAN CHEESE): 222.0 calories; 1.1 g total fat; 0.1 g saturated fat; 8.4 g protein; 45.1 g carbohydrate; 8.0 g dietary fiber; 0 mg cholesterol.

TOTAL PREP TIME: 20 minutes

TOTAL COOKING TIME: 20 to 30 minutes

Preheat the oven to 350°F (180°C, or gas mark 4) and oil an 11-inch (28 cm) tart pan ***or line with parchment paper.

To make the crust, process all the ingredients in a food processor until they resemble cornmeal. Press the crust mixture into the tart pan, patting down with your hand.

To make the filling, add the beans, milk, nutritional yeast, and liquid smoke to a food processor or blender. Process until smooth.

Spread the filling in the tart crust and top with a layer of potato slices. Top with a sprinkling of salt, pepper, and paprika and the vegan cheese. Bake for 20 to 30 minutes or until the potato slices are cooked through.

Serving Suggestions & Variations

Pretty this tart up with thinly sliced purple or red potatoes. Also, you can make the filling creamier by blending ½ cup (120 g) tofu in with it.

Fancy Bean Substitutes: Flageolet, European Solider, Vallarta, Alubia Blanca

Creamy Chickpea and Rice Casserole

▶ GLUTEN-FREE ▶ SOY-FREE OPTION* ▶ OIL-FREE OPTION**

All families love a creamy casserole. This one brings brown rice, mushrooms, and carrots together in a creamy sauce right to your table. The best part is there's very little hands-on time once it goes into the oven to bake for an hour.

1 to 2 tablespoons (15 to 28 ml) olive oil (**use water or broth)

½ small onion, minced

2 cloves garlic, minced

2 cups (140 g) chopped mushrooms

1 cup (130 g) diced carrot (peeled if not organic)

1 cup (100 g) chopped green beans or (130 g) green peas (fresh or frozen)

1½ cups (246 g) cooked chickpeas or 1 can (15 ounces, or 425 g), rinsed and drained

1 tablespoon DIY Poultry Seasoning (page 29)

1 cup (185 g) long-grain brown rice

2½ cups (570 ml) water

2 tablespoons (12 g) nutritional yeast

½ cup (115g) vegan unsweetened yogurt, vegan sour cream, *or Cashew Cream (page 28)

Salt and pepper, to taste

Preheat the oven to 350°F (180°C, or gas mark 4).

Heat the olive oil over medium heat in a Dutch oven or oven-safe pot. Add the onion and sauté until translucent, about 5 minutes. Add the garlic and mushrooms and sauté for 5 minutes more.

Add the carrot, green beans, chickpeas, poultry seasoning, brown rice, and water. Mix well, cover with an oven-safe lid, transfer to the oven, and bake for 60 minutes.

Remove from the oven, add the nutritional yeast and yogurt, and mix well. Taste and add salt and pepper and/or more poultry seasoning if needed.

Fancy Bean Substitutes: Scarlet Runner, Tepary, Good Mother Stallard

YIELD: 4 servings

PER SERVING: 287 calories; 9.4 g total fat; 1.2 g saturated fat; 11.0 g protein; 41.6 g carbohydrate; 8.3 g dietary fiber; 0 mg cholesterol.

TOTAL PREP TIME: 20 minutes

TOTAL COOKING TIME: 65 minutes

Roasted Fall Veggies and Beans

▶ SOY-FREE ▶ GLUTEN-FREE ▶ OIL-FREE OPTION*

This one-dish meal will brighten up your spirits when the days are getting shorter too fast. You can add other veggies to use up bits and pieces you have in the fridge.

1 pound (455 g) brussels sprouts, ends and any yellow leaves removed

1 pound (455 g) cauliflower (about ½ medium head), cut into florets the size of the brussels sprouts

1½ cups (269 g) cooked white beans or 1 can (15 ounces, or 425 g), rinsed and drained

¼ cup (60 ml) balsamic vinegar

¼ cup (60 ml) water

2 teaspoons maple syrup

1 teaspoon Dijon mustard

1 tablespoon olive oil (*omit)

2 (2 inch, or 5 cm) sprigs fresh rosemary or ¼ teaspoon ground

3 (2 inch, or 5 cm) sprigs fresh thyme or 1 teaspoon dried

Salt and pepper, to taste

:::

YIELD: 4 servings

PER SERVING: 163.1 calories; 0.5 g total fat; 0.1 g saturated fat; 10.5 g protein; 32.4 g carbohydrate; 10.6 g dietary fiber; 0 mg cholesterol.

TOTAL PREP TIME: 20 minutes

TOTAL COOKING TIME: 70 to 90 minutes

Preheat the oven to 400°F (200°C, or gas mark 6) and oil a 2-quart (1.8 L) casserole dish or *use a nonstick dish.

If the brussels sprouts are larger than ½ inch (1.3 cm), cut into quarters; otherwise, cut in half. Combine the brussels sprouts, cauliflower, and beans in the casserole dish.

In a small bowl, combine the balsamic vinegar, water, maple syrup, Dijon mustard, and olive oil and pour over the veggies. Bury the herb sprigs in the mixture. If you are using dried herbs, you can mix them into the sauce.

Top with a sprinkling of salt and pepper and bake, covered, for 40 minutes, and then uncover and cook for 30 more minutes.

If the cauliflower is still not done (it is too hard to pierce with a fork), cover and cook an additional 10 to 20 minutes.

Remove the herb stems, taste, and add more salt or pepper if needed.

Fancy Bean Substitutes: Flageolet, European Solider, Vallarta, Alubia Blanca

Tomatillo, Tomato, Black Beans, and Rice

▶ SOY-FREE ▶ GLUTEN-FREE ▶ OIL-FREE OPTION*

This is a super easy weekend dinner that has the wonderful flavors of tomatillos, tomatoes, and cumin. Add chopped seasonal veggies to customize it even more.

1 to 2 tablespoons (15 to 28 ml) olive oil (*use water or broth)

½ small onion, minced

3 cloves garlic, minced

1½ cups (198 g) diced tomatillos (husks removed)

1½ cups (270 g) diced tomatoes or 1 can (14.5 ounces, or 410 g)

1½ cups (258 g) cooked black beans or 1 can (15 ounces, or 425 g), rinsed and drained

1 jalapeño pepper, seeded and minced, or ½ teaspoon jalapeño powder

1 teaspoon smoked paprika

1 teaspoon marjoram

½ teaspoon ground cumin

½ teaspoon chipotle powder

1 cup (185 g) long-grain brown rice

2 cups (475 ml) water

Salt and pepper, to taste

Chopped fresh cilantro, for serving

Hot sauce, for serving

Heat the oil in a large saucepan over medium heat. Add the onion and cook until translucent, about 5 minutes. Add the garlic and sauté another minute or two.

Add the tomatillos, tomatoes, beans, jalapeño, paprika, marjoram, cumin, and chipotle and cover. Cook until the tomatillos break down, about 15 minutes.

Add the rice and water and bring to a boil over high heat. Turn the heat down to low and cover. Cook until the rice is done, 45 to 60 minutes.

Taste and season with salt and pepper. Serve topped with the cilantro and the hot sauce on the side.

Fancy Bean Substitutes: Black Calypso, Vaquero, Purple Runner

:::

YIELD: 4 servings

PER 2-CUP (455 G) SERVING: 219.1 calories; 8.0 g total fat; 1.1 g saturated fat; 5.2 g protein; 31.1 g carbohydrate; 5.4 g dietary fiber; 0 mg cholesterol.

TOTAL PREP TIME: 15 minutes

TOTAL COOKING TIME: 65 to 80 minutes

Chock-Full of Veggies Pot Pie

▶ GLUTEN-FREE OPTION* ▶ SOY-FREE OPTION** ▶ OIL-FREE

You can make one large pie or create mini pies and freeze a few for later.

FOR THE VEGGIES

1½ cups (165 g) diced potatoes (peeled if not organic)

1 cup (130 g) frozen mixed vegetables or a combination of ⅓ cup (51 g) corn, ⅓ cup (43 g) diced carrots, and ⅓ cup (35 g) green beans, cut small

FOR THE SAUCE

2 tablespoons (28 ml) water

¼ cup (18 g) minced mushrooms

2 tablespoons (20 g) minced onion

2 cloves garlic, minced

1 teaspoon marjoram

¼ teaspoon smoked paprika

1 cup (235 ml) unsweetened nondairy milk (**use soy-free)

1 to 2 tablespoons (8 to 16 g) flour *or 1 to 2 teaspoons arrowroot powder

1½ cups (266 g) cooked kidney beans

1 tablespoon (6 g) nutritional yeast

Salt and pepper, to taste

FOR THE CRUST

2 cups (240 g) whole wheat pastry flour (*use gluten-free)

¾ to 1¼ cups (180 to 290 g) unsweetened vegan yogurt (**use plain coconut yogurt)

¾ teaspoon pepper

....

YIELD: 8 servings

PER SERVING: 233.4 calories; 2.3 g total fat; 0.1 g saturated fat; 9.8 g protein; 45.9 g carbohydrate; 9.3 g dietary fiber; 0 mg cholesterol.

TOTAL PREP TIME: 30 minutes

TOTAL COOKING TIME: 45 to 60 minutes

Preheat the oven to 350°F (180°C, or gas mark 4) and oil a 9-inch (23 cm) pie pan ***or line with parchment paper.

To make the veggies, fill a large saucepan halfway with water, add the veggies, and bring to a boil. Lower the heat to a simmer and cook until the potatoes can just be pierced with a fork, about 10 minutes. Drain, rinse under cold water to stop the cooking, and add to a large mixing bowl.

To make the sauce, heat a sauté pan over medium heat and add the water, mushrooms, onion, and garlic. Cook until the mushrooms start to release their liquid and the onion is just starting to brown, about 5 minutes. Add the marjoram, paprika, and milk to the pan. Increase the heat to medium-high and whisk in the flour. You want to reduce the sauce just a bit.

Stir in the beans, nutritional yeast, salt, and pepper and then mix in with the cooked veggies.

To make the crust, add all the ingredients to a food processor and pulse until the yogurt is incorporated and the mixture begins to look like cornmeal. Start with the smaller amount of yogurt and go from there. If your yogurt is thinner, you'll need less than if it is thick. Pour onto a floured cutting board and knead until all the flour is incorporated, just a minute or two.

Divide the dough into 2 equal pieces. Roll one out into a thin circle and place in the pie pan.

Pour the filling into the pie crust. Roll out the other half of the dough and place on top of the filling. Cut any dough that hangs over the pie pan. Go around the pie and crimp the two crusts together with your fingers. Cut a few slits in the top crust with a knife.

Bake for 30 to 45 minutes or until the crust is browned and cooked through.

Cheezy Root Vegetable Bean Bake

▶ SOY-FREE OPTION* ▶ GLUTEN-FREE OPTION** ▶ OIL-FREE OPTION***

There is nothing more comforting than a hearty bowl of potatoes and beans. This recipe adds turnips and rutabagas to the mix to help you use up your winter CSA. Feel free to leave out the ones you don't have on hand and substitute more potatoes.

2 cups (300 g) peeled and diced turnip

2 cups (300 g) peeled and diced rutabaga

2 cups (220 g) diced potato (peeled if not organic)

1½ cups (355 ml) nondairy milk (coconut is my favorite for this) (*use soy-free)

½ cup (48 g) nutritional yeast

½ teaspoon oregano

½ teaspoon thyme

½ teaspoon basil

¼ teaspoon ground rosemary or ½ teaspoon dried

½ teaspoon smoked paprika

2 tablespoons (16 g) flour **or 2 teaspoons arrowroot powder

3 cups (531 g) cooked kidney or pinto beans or 2 cans (15 ounces, or 425 g each), rinsed and drained

Salt and pepper, to taste

Preheat the oven to 350°F (180°C, or gas mark 4) and oil a 2-quart (1.8 L) casserole dish ***or use a nonstick dish.

Fill a large saucepan about halfway with water, add the diced root veggies, and bring to a boil over high heat. Lower the heat to medium after it reaches a rolling boil and cook until the veggies are tender, about 10 minutes. Drain in a colander and then transfer to a large, heat-resistant mixing bowl.

Meanwhile, heat the nondairy milk in a large sauté pan over medium heat and whisk in the nutritional yeast and spices. Heat almost to a boil and then whisk in the flour. Keep whisking and cook until the sauce begins to thicken. Remove from the heat. The sauce will thicken up more as the casserole is baked.

Add the sauce and beans to the bowl with the root veggies and stir to combine. Taste, add salt and pepper, and then transfer to the oiled casserole dish. Bake, covered, for 20 minutes. Remove the cover and bake for 20 more minutes or until the veggies can easily be pierced with a knife.

:::

YIELD: 6 servings

PER 2-CUP (455 G) SERVING: 234.3 calories; 1.3 g total fat; 0.2 g saturated fat; 13.7 g protein; 43.6 g carbohydrate; 9.3 g dietary fiber; 0 mg cholesterol.

TOTAL PREP TIME: 20 minutes

TOTAL COOKING TIME: 60 minutes

Fancy Bean Substitutes: Rio Zape, Goat's Eye, Cranberry

Flageolet Cassoulet

▶ SOY-FREE ▶ OIL-FREE OPTION* ▶ GLUTEN-FREE OPTION**

Imagine an oven-cooked smoky stew topped with crunchy bread crumbs. That's what cassoulet is all about. The flageolet beans are the traditional bean used in this French dish, but any white bean can be substituted.

1 to 2 tablespoons (15 to 28 ml) olive oil (*use water or broth)

½ small onion, minced

5 cloves garlic, chopped

2 stalks celery, chopped, or ½ teaspoon celery seeds

1 large carrot, diced (peeled if not organic)

2 cubes veggie bouillon

5 cups (1.2 L) water

2 Baked Crispy Chickpea Seitan Patties (page 22), cubed, **or 2 cups (496 g) pressed and cubed tofu

1½ cups (322 g) dried flageolet beans or other dried white bean

1 bay leaf

½ teaspoon liquid smoke

4 (2 inch, or 5 cm) sprigs fresh thyme or 1 teaspoon dried

1 (2 inch, or 5 cm) sprig fresh rosemary or ¼ teaspoon ground dried

1 (2 inch, or 5 cm) sprig fresh oregano or ½ teaspoon dried

1 cup (115 g) whole wheat bread crumbs (**use gluten-free)

Salt and pepper, to taste

::

YIELD: 6 servings

PER 1-CUP (225 G) SERVING: 425.4 calories; 6.1 g total fat; 5.6 g saturated fat; 20.0 g protein; 69.7 g carbohydrate; 20.9 g dietary fiber; 0 mg cholesterol.

TOTAL PREP TIME: 20 minutes

TOTAL COOKING TIME: 2 to 2½ hours

Preheat the oven to 350°F (180°C, or gas mark 4).

Heat the oil over medium heat in a Dutch oven. Once hot, add the onion and cook until translucent, about 5 minutes. Add the garlic and celery and cook for 2 minutes. Next add the carrot, bouillon, water, seitan, beans, bay leaf, and liquid smoke. Increase the heat to high and bring to a boil.

Once it's boiling, add the thyme, rosemary, and oregano. Cover and bake for 1½ to 2 hours or until the beans are tender. Check every 40 minutes or so to see whether the beans are ready.

Remove from the oven, remove the bay leaf and herb sprigs, spread the bread crumbs on the top, return to the oven, and bake, uncovered, for 15 more minutes or until the bread crumbs are brown and crispy.

Serving Suggestions & Variations

If you want to use canned white beans instead of dried, use two cans (15 ounces, or 425 g each), rinsed and drained, and reduce the water to 1½ cups (355 ml). Just sauté the veggies and bake for 30 to 45 minutes.

Fancy Bean Substitutes: European Solider, Vallarta, Alubia Blanca

Lentil Quinoa Bolognese Sauce

▶ SOY-FREE ▶ GLUTEN-FREE OPTION*

This hearty, protein-rich sauce serves a crowd, or it can be a staple you make every month or so, freezing any leftovers so they will be there for you during those crazy weeks.

1 cup (192 g) lentils (green, brown, or beluga)

3 medium carrots (peeled if not organic), each cut into 4 large pieces

1 to 2 cups (235 to 475 ml) water

2 tablespoons (28 ml) olive oil

½ small onion, chopped

1 bell pepper, cored, seeded, and chopped

3 cloves garlic, chopped

1 can (20 ounces, or 560 g) crushed tomatoes, or 3 cups (750 g) homemade purée plus 2 teaspoons dried basil

1½ teaspoons dried oregano

1 tablespoon (2 g) dried basil

½ teaspoon red pepper flakes or crushed dried chiles (optional)

1 small bunch kale, stems removed and torn into small pieces (about 3 cups [201 g]) (optional)

½ cup (87 g) quinoa, rinsed well

½ cup (120 ml) red wine or 2 tablespoons (28 ml) balsamic vinegar

Salt and pepper, to taste

Cooked pasta, for serving (*use gluten-free)

Add the lentils, carrots, and water to a large soup pot. Turn the heat to high, cook until the mixture is simmering, and then decrease to low and cover. Cook until the lentils are tender, 20 to 30 minutes.

While the lentils cook, heat the oil in a sauté pan over medium heat. Add the onion and sauté until translucent, about 5 minutes. Then add the bell pepper and garlic and sauté for 1 minute more.

Once the carrots and lentils are cooked remove the carrots from the pot of lentils and add them to a food processor or blender along with the tomatoes, oregano, basil, red pepper flakes, kale, and sautéed veggies, and purée until smooth.

At the same time, add the quinoa and red wine to the pot of lentils. Turn the heat to medium, cook until it starts to simmer again, and then cover and decrease the heat to low. Cook until the quinoa start to show their white tails.

Add the purée to the lentil-quinoa mixture and cook, covered, over low heat until the sauce melds and heats thoroughly, about 20 minutes.

:::

YIELD: 8 servings

PER 1½-CUP (340 G) SERVING: 157.1 calories; 3.0 g total fat; 0.3 g saturated fat; 6.8 g protein; 26.3 g carbohydrate; 6.2 g dietary fiber; 0 mg cholesterol.

TOTAL PREP TIME: 20 minutes

TOTAL COOKING TIME: 40 to 60 minutes

Sun-Dried Tomato White Bean Wheat Balls

▶ SOY-FREE ▶ OIL-FREE OPTION*

I always keep a batch of these in the freezer for quick and easy wheat ball subs or to stretch a pasta dish when unexpected guests come over. The wheat gluten gives them a meaty texture and the sun-dried tomato bits make little flavor explosions in your mouth. Serve on top of pasta covered with pasta sauce or in a hoagie roll covered with tomato sauce and shredded Daiya mozzarella.

¼ cup (14 g) sun-dried tomatoes

1½ cups (358 g) cooked white beans or 1 can (15 ounces, or 425 g), rinsed and drained

¼ to ½ cup (60 to 120 ml) water or broth

¼ cup (36 g) almonds

1 cup (120 g) vital wheat gluten flour

3 tablespoons (18 g) nutritional yeast

1 teaspoon dried basil

1 teaspoon dried oregano

½ teaspoon garlic powder or 2 cloves, minced

Salt and pepper (I used smoked salt), to taste

¼ to ½ cup (24 to 47 g) oat bran, bread crumbs, or (29 to 58 g) wheat germ

....

YIELD: 24 balls

PER BALL: 47.5 calories; 0.8 g total fat; 0.1 g saturated fat; 5.7 g protein; 5.4 g carbohydrate; 2.1 g dietary fiber; 0 mg cholesterol.

TOTAL PREP TIME: 20 minutes

TOTAL COOKING TIME: 20 to 25 minutes

Preheat the oven to 375°F (190°C, or gas mark 5). Grease a sheet pan *or line with parchment paper.

In a food processor, pulverize the sun-dried tomatoes (or purée if they are packed in oil). Add the beans and ¼ cup (60 ml) of the water and purée.

Add the rest of the ingredients except the oat bran and process until well combined. Add the remaining ¼ cup (60 ml) water if needed, but leave it out if the mixture is just right. At this point you want to be able to knead the mixture and roll it into balls.

Spread ¼ cup (24 g) of the oat bran on a cutting board. Top with ball mixture and knead for a minute or two until all of the dough is the same consistency.

Cut the dough into 24 similar-size pieces. I use a dough cutter, but a dinner knife works just fine. Roll into balls. Spread the remaining ¼ cup (24 g) oat bran on the cutting board and roll the balls in it.

Place the balls on the prepared pan and bake for 15 minutes. Turn them over and bake for 5 to 10 minutes more.

Fancy Bean Substitutes: Flageolet, European Solider, Vallarta, Alubia Blanca

Baked Beany Mac and Cheezy

▶ SOY-FREE OPTION* ▶ GLUTEN-FREE OPTION** ▶ OIL-FREE OPTION***

This is a mac and cheese you can feel good about serving your family. The turnip mimics the sharpness of cheese, puréed white beans create the base of the no-cream sauce, and the carrots color it orange and add a bit of sweetness.

2 carrots, cut into large pieces

3 small salad turnips, left unpeeled, or 1 small regular turnip, peeled, cut into large pieces

2 cups (210 g) uncooked whole wheat macaroni (**use gluten-free)

1½ cups (358 g) cooked white beans or 1 can (15 ounces, or 425 g), rinsed and drained

1 cup (235 ml) unsweetened nondairy milk (*use soy-free)

¼ cup (24 g) nutritional yeast

1 teaspoon dried basil

1 clove garlic, minced

½ teaspoon smoked paprika

Salt and pepper, to taste

¾ cup (86 g) whole wheat bread crumbs (**use gluten-free)

½ cup (50 g) Easy Almond Parm (page 27) or store-bought vegan Parmesan cheese

Preheat the oven to 350°F (180°C, or gas mark 4). Oil a casserole dish ***or use a nonstick pan.

Add the carrots and turnips to a saucepan, cover with water, and cook over medium heat until easily pierced with a fork, 10 to 15 minutes.

While the veggies are cooking, bring a large saucepan of water to a boil. Cook the pasta about 3 minutes less than the directions on the package. Drain and set aside.

In a food processor, combine the beans, milk, nutritional yeast, basil, garlic, smoked paprika, and cooked veggies. Purée until smooth. Taste and season with salt and pepper.

Give the pasta a quick rinse under cold water to wash away the starch and keep it from sticking together. Add to a mixing bowl, pour the sauce over, stir to combine, and then transfer to the prepared casserole dish.

Bake for 20 minutes and then top with the bread crumbs and some of the almond parm. Bake until the topping is crisp, 15 to 20 minutes.

....

YIELD: 4 servings

PER 2-CUP (455 G) SERVING: 315.4 calories; 3.1 g total fat; 0.2 g saturated fat; 16.9 g protein; 59.5 g carbohydrate; 16.2 g dietary fiber; 0 mg cholesterol.

TOTAL PREP TIME: 20 minutes

TOTAL COOKING TIME: 55 to 65 minutes

Fancy Bean Substitutes: Flageolet, European Solider, Vallarta, Alubia Blanca

Eggplant White Bean Pasta Sauce

▶ SOY-FREE OPTION* ▶ GLUTEN-FREE ▶ OIL-FREE OPTION**

You make this hearty pasta sauce in the oven. No stirring is needed, so it cooks while you do other chores around the house. It freezes great.

1 can (28 ounces, or 785 g) crushed tomatoes with basil or 3 cups (540 g) diced fresh tomatoes with their juice

¼ cup (24 g) nutritional yeast

¼ cup (60 ml) unsweetened nondairy milk (*use soy-free)

2 tablespoons (5 g) chopped fresh basil

2 teaspoons thyme

1 teaspoon oregano

½ teaspoon ground rosemary

Salt and pepper, to taste

3 cups (537 g) cooked white beans or 2 cans (15 ounces, or 425 g each), rinsed and drained

3 cups (246 g) finely diced eggplant

::

YIELD: 10 cups (2.5 kg)

PER 1-CUP (225 G) SERVING: 136.8 calories; 0.7 g total fat; 0.1 g saturated fat; 9.0 g protein; 26.0 g carbohydrate; 6.7 g dietary fiber; 0 mg cholesterol.

TOTAL PREP TIME: 20 minutes

TOTAL COOKING TIME: 60 minutes

Preheat the oven to 350°F (180°C, or gas mark 4). Oil an 11 x 8-inch (28 x 20 cm) casserole pan **or use a nonstick pan.

Combine everything except the beans and eggplant in a large mixing bowl. Add salt and pepper to taste. Stir in the beans and eggplant, mix well, and then spread in the casserole pan and cover with foil. Bake for 60 minutes until the eggplant is tender.

Serving Suggestions & Variations

You could make this in the slow cooker, but the beans will break down more. If that's okay with you, cook on low for 8 to 9 hours.

Fancy Bean Substitutes: Flageolet, European Solider, Vallarta, Alubia Blanca

White Bean Lemon Basil Stuffed Shells

▶ SOY-FREE OPTION* ▶ GLUTEN-FREE OPTION** ▶ OIL-FREE OPTION***

These are a great weekend dinner. You can double the recipe and freeze the second batch for a quick weeknight dinner. I love the extra lemony flavor of lemon basil, but you can use any basil.

3 cups (537 g) cooked white beans or 2 cans (15 ounces, or 425 g each), rinsed and drained

½ cup (120 ml) unsweetened nondairy milk (*use soy-free)

½ cup (20 g) chopped fresh basil (try lemon basil), thyme, or arugula

¼ cup (24 g) nutritional yeast

Salt and pepper, to taste

1 can (28 ounces, or 785 g) crushed tomatoes (with basil, if possible) or 3 cups (540 g) diced fresh

1 teaspoon oregano

½ teaspoon ground rosemary

½ teaspoon granulated garlic or 1 clove garlic, minced

20 large pasta shells, cooked and cooled (**use gluten-free)

Preheat the oven to 350°F (180°C, or gas mark 4). Oil an 11 x 8-inch (28 x 20 cm) casserole pan ***or use a nonstick pan.

Put the beans, milk, basil, and nutritional yeast in a food processor and process until smooth. Season with salt and pepper. This is your shell filling.

In a bowl, combine the crushed tomatoes and herbs. This will be your sauce. You can substitute bottled or home-made pasta sauce in its place.

Spread half of the tomato sauce on the bottom of the prepared pan. Take each shell and add a heaping table-spoon (15 g) of filling and place in the pan. Repeat until the pan is full and all the shells have been used.

Spread the rest of the sauce over the top, cover with foil, and bake until heated through, about 30 minutes.

::

YIELD: 20 shells

PER SHELL: 103 calories; 0.6 g total fat; 0.2 g saturated fat; 5.4 g protein; 19.6 g carbohydrate; 2.9 g dietary fiber; 0 mg cholesterol.

TOTAL PREP TIME: 25 minutes

TOTAL COOKING TIME: 30 minutes

Fancy Bean Substitutes: Flageolet, European Solider, Vallarta, Alubia Blanca

Chickpea and Vegetable Lo Mein

▶ SOY-FREE OPTION* ▶ GLUTEN-FREE OPTION** ▶ OIL-FREE

This is stay-in food at its easiest. Make a pineapple ginger garlic sauce, boil the pasta and a few veggies, and then the rest gets a quick sauté in a wok or large sauté pan.

FOR THE SAUCE

1 tablespoon (8 g) grated ginger

3 cloves garlic, minced

½ cup (85 g) pineapple chunks

1 cup (235 ml) pineapple juice

2 tablespoons (28 ml) soy sauce (use *coconut aminos or **gluten-free soy sauce)

1 tablespoon (15 ml) rice wine vinegar or brown rice vinegar

FOR THE LO MEIN

8 ounces (225 g) whole wheat spaghetti (**use gluten-free)

2 carrots, julienned (peeled if not organic)

2 cups (142 g) broccoli florets

1 cup (120 g) chopped summer squash

1 stalk celery, julienned

½ bell pepper, cored, seeded, and chopped

2 cups (140 g) shredded cabbage

1½ cups (246 g) cooked chickpeas or 1 can (15 ounces, or 425 g), rinsed and drained

....

YIELD: 4 servings

PER 2-CUP (455 G) SERVING: 398.0 calories; 3.6 g total fat; 0.2 g saturated fat; 14.5 g protein; 86.3 g carbohydrate; 14.3 g dietary fiber; 0 mg cholesterol.

TOTAL PREP TIME: 20 minutes

TOTAL COOKING TIME: 45 minutes

Bring a pot of water to a boil over high heat.

To make the sauce, add all the ingredients to a food processor and purée until smooth.

Once the water is boiling, add the pasta and carrots. Lower the heat to medium-high and cook pasta according to the package directions. Add the broccoli about 3 minutes before the pasta is done. You want to precook it just a bit because it will cook more in the sauce. Cook until the pasta is al dente or the way you like it. Drain the pasta and veggies.

Heat a large sauté pan or wok over medium heat, add the sauce, summer squash, celery, bell pepper, and cabbage. Cook for about 10 minutes, then add the cooked pasta, carrots, broccoli, and chickpeas, and stir to combine and heat through, about 10 minutes.

Serving Suggestions & Variations

Switch up the sauce by adding red pepper flakes or sriracha to spice it up, or change out the pineapple for orange chunks and orange juice for another variation.

Fancy Bean Substitutes: Scarlet Runner, Tepary, Good Mother Stallard

Brown Rice Fava Bean Risotto

▶ SOY-FREE ▶ GLUTEN-FREE ▶ OIL-FREE OPTION*

Short-grain brown rice is starchy enough to make a risotto. It will not be exactly the same as the traditional one, but it's awfully close. Just vary the veggies (and type of bean) to match the season and eat this all year-round.

3 veggie bouillon cubes

6 to 7 cups (1.4 L to 1.6 L) water

1 to 2 tablespoons (15 to 28 ml) olive oil (*use water or broth)

½ small onion, minced

2 cloves garlic, minced

1 cup (190 g) short-grain brown rice

2 or 3 medium carrots, sliced (peeled if not organic)

¼ cup (38 g) minced red bell pepper

1½ teaspoons oregano

1½ teaspoons marjoram

1 cup (170 g) frozen fava beans

½ teaspoon lemon zest

Salt and pepper, to taste

:::

YIELD: 4 servings

PER 1-CUP (225 G) SERVING: 202.0 calories; 7.9 g total fat; 1.0 g saturated fat; 6.0 g protein; 27.5 g carbohydrate; 6.3 g dietary fiber; 0 mg cholesterol.

TOTAL PREP TIME: 20 minutes

TOTAL COOKING TIME: 60 minutes for stove top, or 1½ to 2½ hours for slow cooker

STOVE-TOP DIRECTIONS*

Dissolve the bouillon cubes in 6 cups (1.4 L) of the water to make broth.

Heat the olive oil in a soup pot over medium heat. Add the onion and sauté until translucent, about 5 minutes. Add the garlic, rice, carrots, bell pepper, oregano, and marjoram. Sauté for 2 or 3 minutes more.

Now start adding the broth ½ cup (120 ml) at a time, stirring continuously. You will continue doing this throughout the cooking process, which will take about 1 hour.

At about the 30-minute mark, add the fava beans and lemon zest. Add the broth ½ cup (120 ml) at a time until the rice is cooked but still has a bit of a bite. The favas and carrots should be cooked at this point, too. Add some or all of the remaining 1 cup (235 ml) water if needed.

Taste and season with salt and pepper or more herbs.

SLOW COOKER DIRECTIONS

Heat the olive oil over medium heat in a soup pot. Add the onion and sauté until translucent, about 5 minutes.

Oil the crock of a slow cooker and add everything except for the lemon zest, salt, and pepper. Cook on high for 1½ to 2½ hours. Stir every 20 to 30 minutes, adding extra water if needed. Adjust the herbs and season with salt and pepper.

Fancy Bean Substitutes: Scarlet Runner, Christmas Lima, Good Mother Stallard

Summer Solstice Oven Pesto Risotto (with Winter Variation)

▶ SOY-FREE ▶ GLUTEN-FREE ▶ OIL-FREE OPTION*

This easy, no-stir risotto is full of garden-fresh veggies. The pesto really adds a burst of flavor. Making it in the oven means no stirring and no standing over a hot stove!

1 to 2 tablespoons (15 to 28 ml) olive oil (*use water or broth)

½ small onion, minced

2 cloves garlic, minced

2½ cups (570 ml) water

½ cup (120 ml) white wine or more water

1½ cups (345 g) Arborio rice

1 medium zucchini or yellow squash, cut into chunks

1 cup (150 g) cherry tomatoes, cut in half or quarters

1 cup (164 g) corn kernels

1 cup (82 g) Japanese eggplant chunks

1½ cups (246 g) cooked chickpeas or 1 can (15 ounces, or 425 g), rinsed and drained

¼ to ½ teaspoon black pepper

FOR THE PESTO SAUCE

1 packed cup (24 g) fresh basil leaves

3 tablespoons (45 ml) water

2 tablespoons (12 g) nutritional yeast

Salt, to taste

:::

YIELD: 6 servings

PER 1½-CUP (340 G) SERVING: 319.4 calories; 5.7 g total fat; 0.7 g saturated fat; 8.6 g protein; 54.4 g carbohydrate; 6.8 g dietary fiber; 0 mg cholesterol.

TOTAL PREP TIME: 20 minutes

TOTAL COOKING TIME: 40 to 50 minutes

Preheat the oven to 350°F (180°C, or gas mark 4).

Heat the olive oil in a Dutch oven or other oven-safe pan over medium heat. Add the onion and cook until translucent, about 5 minutes. Add the garlic and then sauté another minute or two more.

Add the water, wine, and rice and turn the heat up to high. Once it begins to boil, remove from the heat and stir in the veggies, chickpeas, and black pepper.

Cover and put into oven for 35 to 45 minutes or until the rice is al dente. You don't want to overcook it because it will get mushy.

Meanwhile, to make the pesto sauce, put all the ingredients except the salt into a food processor and purée. Taste and add salt. You want the sauce to be looser than a typical pesto so that it's easy to mix into the risotto.

Once the rice is done, remove it from the oven and stir in the pesto. Adjust salt and pepper as needed.

Serving Suggestions & Variations

• Make this whole grain by using short-grain brown rice.

• Use winter squash, turnips, sweet potato, or even rutabagas to winterize this dish.

Fancy Bean Substitutes: Scarlet Runner, Tepary, Good Mother Stallard

Eggplant Lasagna with White Bean Basil Spread

▶ SOY-FREE OPTION* ▶ GLUTEN-FREE OPTION** ▶ OIL-FREE OPTION***

This is easy to whip up when a lasagna craving hits. You can add 1 cup (248 g) tofu to the filling to make it more ricotta-like.

FOR THE SAUCE

1 can (28 ounces, or 785 g) crushed tomatoes (with basil, if possible) or 3 cups (540 g) diced fresh

1 teaspoon oregano

¼ teaspoon ground rosemary or 1 teaspoon dried leaves

Salt and pepper, to taste

FOR THE FILLING

2 recipes White Bean Basil Cheezy Spread (page 54)

½ cup (120 ml) unsweetened nondairy milk (*use soy-free)

1 medium eggplant, thinly sliced

1 package (9 ounces, or 255 g) whole wheat lasagna noodles (**use gluten-free)

::

YIELD: 8 servings

PER SERVING: 233.5 calories; 1.9 g total fat; 0.1 g saturated fat; 12.3 g protein; 50.4 g carbohydrate; 12.4 g dietary fiber; 0 mg cholesterol.

TOTAL PREP TIME: 25 minutes

TOTAL COOKING TIME: 60 minutes

Preheat the oven to 350°F (180°C, or gas mark 4). Oil an 11 x 8-inch (28 x 20 cm) casserole pan ***or use a nonstick pan.

To make the sauce, combine all the ingredients together in a mixing bowl.

To make the filling, add the white bean spread and non-dairy milk to a food processor and blend; this will make it easier to spread.

Layer some sauce on the bottom of the prepared pan, arrange a layer of the eggplant, top that with a layer of the noodles, and follow that with the white bean filling. Repeat the layers. Finally, top with one more layer of eggplant, noodles, and sauce. Cover with foil and bake for 60 minutes or until the center is steaming.

Fancy Bean Substitutes: Flageolet, European Solider, Vallarta, Alubia Blanca

Creamy Healthified Vodka Sauce

▶ SOY-FREE OPTION* ▶ OIL-FREE ▶ GLUTEN-FREE OPTION**

This creamy, pink pasta sauce comes together quickly and feels like a decadent treat, but it's really good for you.

1½ cups (358 g) cooked white beans or 1 can (15 ounces, or 425 g), rinsed and drained

1½ cups (270 g) diced fresh tomatoes or 1 can (14.5 ounces, or 410 g)

1 cup (235 ml) unsweetened nondairy milk (*use soy-free)

⅓ cup (80 ml) vodka

2 cloves garlic

2 tablespoons (12 g) nutritional yeast

¼ teaspoon red pepper flakes

Salt and pepper, to taste

6 cups (840 g) cooked whole wheat pasta, for serving (**use gluten-free)

Handful of fresh basil, cut into ribbons

Add the white beans, tomatoes, nondairy milk, vodka, garlic, nutritional yeast, and red pepper flakes to a food processor and purée until smooth.

Pour into a saucepan and cook over medium heat, stirring, for 10 to 15 minutes, until heated through. Season with salt and pepper. Serve over cooked pasta and topped with fresh basil.

Fancy Bean Substitutes: Flageolet, European Solider, Vallarta, Alubia Blanca

:::

YIELD: 6 servings

PER ½-CUP (115 G) SERVING (DOES NOT INCLUDE PASTA): 274 calories; 0.9 g total fat; 0.2 g saturated fat; 13.0 g protein; 49.8 g carbohydrate; 9.5 g dietary fiber; 0 mg cholesterol.

TOTAL PREP TIME: 10 minutes

TOTAL COOKING TIME: 10 to 15 minutes

Coconut Thai Basil Rice Noodles with Tofu or Chickpeas

▶ SOY-FREE OPTION* ▶ GLUTEN-FREE OPTION**

These creamy noodles are perfect hot or cold, so they go with every season!

1 package (8.8 ounces, or 249 g) thin rice noodles (sometimes known as mai fun)

1 package (15.5 ounces, or 439 g) tofu, pressed for at least 15 minutes and up to overnight, then cut into small cubes (*or 3 cups [492 g] cooked chickpeas or 2 cans [15 ounces, or 425 g each], rinsed and drained)

FOR THE SAUCE

1 cup (24 g) fresh Thai basil leaves

2 cloves garlic, minced

Zest and juice of 1 lime

1 can (14 ounces, or 400 ml) light coconut milk

2 tablespoons (28 ml) soy sauce (use *coconut aminos or **gluten-free soy sauce)

½ teaspoon tamarind paste

1 teaspoon sriracha (**use gluten-free)

Bring a large pot of water to a boil, add the rice noodles, and then remove from the heat. They will be cooked in about 8 to 10 minutes. Drain in a colander.

Brown the tofu in a hot sauté pan or wok or bake it in a 350°F (180°C, or gas mark 4) oven in an oiled pan for about 15 minutes per side to make it firm and lightly browned. You want it to have a bit of texture. (Warm up the chickpeas if you are making the soy-free version.)

To make the sauce, purée all the ingredients in a food processor or blender. In a large bowl (or the pot you cooked the noodles in), mix the sauce with the noodles.

Serve the sauced noodles in bowls topped with the warm tofu or chickpeas.

Fancy Bean Substitutes: Scarlet Runner, Tepary, Good Mother Stallard

YIELD: 8 servings

PER 2-CUP (455 G) SERVING: 502.0 calories; 5.6 g total fat; 2.7 g saturated fat; 6.1 g protein; 109 g carbohydrate; 0.4 g dietary fiber; 0 mg cholesterol.

TOTAL PREP TIME: 15 minutes

TOTAL COOKING TIME: 20 to 30 minutes

Stove-Top Mac 'n Beany

▶ SOY-FREE OPTION* ▶ OIL-FREE ▶ GLUTEN-FREE OPTION**

This mac 'n cheez is a perfect quick weeknight meal. However, if I know I'm making it the next day, I'll go ahead and cook the carrots and keep them in the fridge until I'm ready to use them. You could cook them a few days before if you've made a menu plan.

1½ cups (269 g) cooked white beans or 1 can (15 ounces, or 425 g), rinsed and drained

2 small carrots, cut into large chunks (peeled if not organic) and cooked until tender

1 cup (235 ml) unsweetened nondairy milk, plus extra if needed (*use soy-free)

¼ cup (35 g) cashews (optional)

½ cup (48 g) nutritional yeast

1 teaspoon Dijon mustard

½ teaspoon granulated garlic or 2 cloves, minced

½ teaspoon turmeric

¼ to ½ teaspoon liquid smoke (optional)

Salt and pepper, to taste

16 ounces (455 g) dried elbow pasta, for serving (**use gluten-free)

Add everything except the pasta, salt, and pepper to a food processor or blender and purée until smooth. Taste and season with salt and pepper.

Meanwhile, bring a pot of water to a boil, add the pasta, and cook according to package directions until al dente. Drain in a colander and set aside. Warm the sauce in the same pot so there is less clean-up later. After the sauce is warm, add the drained pasta and mix well. Add extra nondairy milk, if needed. Taste and adjust the salt and pepper one more time.

Serving Suggestions & Variations

The cashews are optional, so don't fret if you have a nut allergy! They do add more creaminess, but the dish works fine without them, too.

Fancy Bean Substitutes: Black Calypso, Vaquero, Purple Runner, European Solider, Vallarta, Alubia Blanca

:::

YIELD: 6 servings

PER 1½-CUP (340 G) SERVING: 403.0 calories; 7.6 g total fat; 0.7 g saturated fat; 14.8 g protein; 74.5 g carbohydrate; 15.2 g dietary fiber; 0 mg cholesterol.

TOTAL PREP TIME: 15 minutes

TOTAL COOKING TIME: 10 to 15 minutes

Super Easy Lentil Biryani

▶ SOY-FREE ▶ GLUTEN-FREE ▶ OIL-FREE

If you've had the longest day ever and still need to make dinner, this is the recipe for you. Throw everything into a pan or your rice cooker and dinner will be ready in no time!

1½ cups (279 g) brown basmati rice

4 cups (950 ml) water, plus more if needed

½ cup (96 g) lentils

¼ cup (35 g) chopped cashews

¼ cup (35 g) raisins

¼ cup (33 g) minced dried apricots

2 teaspoons minced ginger

½ teaspoon turmeric

2 cloves garlic, minced

2 bay leaves

2 cinnamon sticks or ½ teaspoon ground

3 black cardamom pods or ½ teaspoon ground

4 whole cloves or ¼ teaspoon ground

8 whole black peppercorns or ¼ teaspoon ground

10 coriander seeds or 1 teaspoon ground

½ teaspoon garam masala

¼ teaspoon salt

STOVE-TOP DIRECTIONS

Put all the ingredients except the salt into a large saucepan and bring to a boil over high heat. Cover and decrease the heat to low and cook until the rice and lentils are tender, 40 to 50 minutes. Check after 30 minutes and add more water if needed.

Add the salt and adjust other seasonings if needed and remove the bay leaves, cinnamon sticks, and cardamom pods before serving.

RICE COOKER DIRECTIONS

The two differences between cooking this on the stove top and in your rice cooker is that you will use 2 cups (380 g) brown basmati rice (use the measuring cup that came with your rice cooker) and add water to fill line 2 in your rice cooker plus 1 cup (235 ml) water in a regular measuring cup.

Put all the ingredients into the rice cooker and cook on the brown rice setting if you have one.

When your rice cooker beeps, taste, add salt, and taste again. Adjust the other seasonings if needed and remove the bay leaves, cinnamon sticks, and cardamom pods before serving.

::

YIELD: 4 servings

PER 1½-CUP (340 G) SERVING: 377.0 calories; 5.0 g total fat; 0.5 g saturated fat; 10.0 g protein; 76.5 g carbohydrate; 7.5 g dietary fiber; 0 mg cholesterol.

TOTAL PREP TIME: 10 minutes

TOTAL COOKING TIME: 40 to 60 minutes (until your rice cooker beeps)

New Orleans Red Bean Jambalaya

▶ GLUTEN-FREE ▶ OIL-FREE OPTION* ▶ SOY-FREE OPTION**

This rice and bean dish brings New Orleans to your table and can be made with staples you already have around the house. I love to use smoked tempeh in this, but you can use a little liquid smoke instead and get the same flavor. This dish is a great way to use up bits of leftover veggies.

1 to 2 tablespoons (15 to 28 ml) olive oil (*use water or broth)

1 small onion, minced

2 stalks celery, minced, or ½ teaspoon celery seeds

4 cloves garlic, minced

1 medium bell pepper, cored, seeded, and chopped

1 tablespoon Cajun Spice Blend (page 29)

1½ cups (270 g) diced tomatoes or 1 can (14.5 ounces, or 410 g)

1½ cups (266 g) cooked kidney beans or 1 can (15 ounces, or 425 g), rinsed and drained

8 ounces (225 g) smoked tempeh (**or use double the amount of beans and add ½ teaspoon liquid smoke)

2 cups (weight will vary) chopped seasonal veggies, such as summer squash, greens, eggplant, and winter squash

2 veggie bouillon cubes

3 cups (700 ml) water

1½ cups (278 g) brown rice

Salt and pepper, to taste

Tabasco or other hot sauce, for serving

Heat the olive oil over medium heat in a large soup pot. Add the onion and cook until translucent, about 5 minutes. Add the celery, garlic, and bell pepper and sauté another 3 minutes.

Add the rest of the ingredients except the salt, pepper, and Tabasco. Turn the heat to medium-high and bring almost to a boil.

Turn the heat down to low and cover. Cook until the rice is done, about 30 to 45 minutes. Stir every 20 minutes and add more liquid if needed.

Once the rice is ready, season with salt and pepper. Add more Cajun seasoning if needed. I serve the hot sauce on the side because of picky eaters in my household, but feel free to add some in and serve more on the side.

Fancy Bean Substitutes: Rio Zape, Goat's Eye, Cranberry

YIELD: 6 servings

PER 1½-CUP (340 G) SERVING: 294.0 calories; 10.0 g total fat; 1.7 g saturated fat; 15.2 g protein; 39.0 g carbohydrate; 8.4 g dietary fiber; 0 mg cholesterol.

TOTAL PREP TIME: 20 minutes

TOTAL COOKING TIME: 35 to 50 minutes

Super Simple Mexican Quinoa with Black Beans

▶ SOY-FREE ▶ GLUTEN-FREE ▶ OIL-FREE OPTION*

This is a recipe that's good as is. However, you can add extra seasonal veggies, tempeh, seitan, or tofu or even change the spices. Think of this as a starting point and see where your creativity takes you.

1½ cups (225 g) chopped bell pepper

3 cloves garlic, minced

1½ cups (355 ml) water

1½ cups (270 g) diced tomatoes or 1 can (14.5 ounces, or 410 g), undrained

1½ cups (258 g) cooked black beans or 1 can (15 ounces, or 425 g), rinsed and drained

1 cube vegetable bouillon

1 to 2 teaspoons chili powder

½ teaspoon ground cumin

¾ cup (128 g) quinoa, rinsed well

Salt and pepper, to taste

....

YIELD: 4 servings

PER 1½-CUP (340 G) SERVING: 254.3 calories; 2.6 g total fat; 0.1 g saturated fat; 11.6 g protein; 46.5 g carbohydrate; 9.3 g dietary fiber; 0 mg cholesterol.

TOTAL PREP TIME: 15 minutes

TOTAL COOKING TIME: 20 minutes for stove top, 6 to 10 hours for slow cooker

STOVE-TOP DIRECTIONS*
Add all the ingredients except the salt and pepper to a medium saucepot with a lid. Bring to a boil over high heat and then decrease the heat to low and cook for 15 minutes or until the tails unravel on the quinoa. That's the signal that they're ready to eat.

Season with salt and pepper. Taste and add more chili powder or cumin, if needed.

SLOW COOKER DIRECTIONS
The night before: Prepare the veggies and rinse the beans if you are using canned and keep in the fridge overnight.

In the morning: Add everything except the quinoa to an oiled slow cooker. Increase the amount of water to 2½ cups (570 ml). Cook on low for 6 to 10 hours. (You will add the quinoa later.)

About 1 to 2 hours before serving: Turn the slow cooker to high and add the quinoa. Cook until you see the quinoa's tails unravel, about 20 minutes. That's the signal that they're ready to eat. Taste and add salt, more cumin, extra chili powder—whatever you need to do to make it the way you like it!

Fancy Bean Substitutes: Black Calypso, Vaquero, Purple Runner

Linda Watson's Adzuki Beans

▶ SOY-FREE ▶ GLUTEN-FREE ▶ OIL-FREE OPTION*

My friend Linda Watson is the author of *Wildly Affordable Organic*. We meet almost every week to talk about what we're cooking up. Be sure to take a look at her site, www.cookforgood.com.

2 cloves garlic, minced

1 pound (455 g) dried adzuki beans or 4½ cups (1 kg) cooked or 3 cans (15 ounces, or 425 g each), rinsed and drained

1 large onion, chopped

1 to 2 teaspoons salt

1 carrot, sliced into ¼-inch (6 mm) coins (peeled if not organic)

6 cups (1.4 L) water

FOR THE ORANGE SAUCE

2 teaspoons sesame, peanut, or canola oil (*use water or broth)

2 cloves garlic, minced

2 teaspoons grated ginger

½ teaspoon chipotle or cayenne powder

1 large onion, chopped

4 cups (280 g) shredded green cabbage or 2 bell peppers, cored, and thinly sliced into bite-size pieces

Zest and juice of 2 oranges

About 5 cups (975 g) cooked brown rice, for serving

1 orange, cut into wedges, for garnish

Put the garlic, adzuki beans, onion, salt, carrot, and water into a soup pot. Cover the pot, bring to a boil over high heat, and then reduce the heat to a low simmer and cook for 1½ to 2 hours. This is when the beans will just start to become tender, which is when it's time to make the sauce. (This could take longer if your beans are older.)

To make the sauce, heat the sesame oil in a large skillet over medium-low heat. Add the garlic, ginger, and chipotle powder and cook until fragrant, about 20 seconds. Add the onion, stir, and cook until soft, about 5 minutes.

Add the cabbage and orange zest and juice to the onion mixture, stir to combine, and cook until the cabbage is tender, 5 to 10 minutes more.

Meanwhile, if the beans are too watery, you can either drain them or remove the lid and allow the extra liquid to evaporate.

Spoon the beans over the rice, ladle the sauce on top, and garnish with the orange wedges.

:::

YIELD: 10 servings

PER ¾-CUP (170 G) SAUCE (DOES NOT INCLUDE RICE): 178.3 calories; 1.3 g total fat; 0.1 g saturated fat; 9.0 g protein; 34.4 g carbohydrate; 7.3 g dietary fiber; 0 mg cholesterol.

TOTAL PREP TIME: 20 minutes

TOTAL COOKING TIME: 1½ to 2 hours

Jamaican Purple Hull Peas and Rice

▶ SOY-FREE ▶ GLUTEN-FREE ▶ OIL-FREE OPTION*

Purple hull peas, pigeon peas, and cowpeas are all crowder peas. They are unique in that their shells are not edible. However, this peas-and-rice dish is very edible and full of bold flavors.

1 to 2 tablespoons (15 to 28 ml) olive oil (*use water or broth)

½ small onion, minced

2 cloves garlic, minced

1 teaspoon grated ginger

1½ cups (308 g) purple hull peas or pigeon peas, fresh or frozen

1½ cups (355 ml) water

1 can (14 ounces, or 400 ml) light coconut milk

3 (2 inch, or 5 cm) sprigs fresh thyme or 1 teaspoon dried

¼ teaspoon allspice

¼ teaspoon habanero powder

1 cube veggie bouillon

¼ teaspoon lime zest

1½ cups (278 g) long-grain red, brown, or white rice

Salt and pepper, to taste

Heat the olive oil over medium heat in a soup pot. Add the onion and sauté until translucent, about 5 minutes. Add the garlic and ginger and sauté for an additional 2 or 3 minutes.

Add the rest of the ingredients except the salt and pepper. Bring to a boil over high heat and then turn the heat to low and cover. Cook for 20 to 45 minutes or until the rice is ready. If you use white or red rice, it will be closer to 20 minutes, and if you use brown rice, it will take up to 45 minutes. Taste and season with salt and pepper.

Fancy Bean Substitutes: Flageolet, Yellow-Eyed Peas, Adzuki

YIELD: 6 servings

PER 1½-CUP (340 G) SERVING: 318.1 calories; 10.5 g total fat; 4.3 g saturated fat; 8.3 g protein; 48.3 g carbohydrate; 4.7 g dietary fiber; 0 mg cholesterol.

TOTAL PREP TIME: 15 minutes

TOTAL COOKING TIME: 20 to 45 minutes

Pineapple Fried Rice

▶ SOY-FREE OPTION* ▶ GLUTEN-FREE OPTION** ▶ OIL-FREE OPTION***

This is my favorite way to use leftover rice. Chock full of veggies and pineapple and either edamame or chickpeas, it makes for a quick meal.

FOR THE SAUCE

4 tablespoons (32 g) grated ginger

6 cloves garlic, minced

1 teaspoon tamarind paste

2 tablespoons (28 ml) soy sauce (use *coconut aminos or **gluten-free soy sauce)

2 tablespoons (28 ml) water

FOR THE RICE

1 to 2 tablespoons (15 to 28 ml) sesame oil (***use water or broth)

½ small onion, minced

1 bell pepper, cored, seeded, and minced

2 cups (330 g) pineapple chunks

1 pound (455 g) shelled edamame (*use chickpeas)

1 can (15 ounces, or 425 g) baby corn, rinsed and drained

1 cup (150 g) green peas, fresh or frozen

6 cups (1.2 kg) cold cooked brown rice

To make the sauce, in a small bowl, mix the ingredients together and set aside.

Heat the oil in a large sauté pan or wok over medium-high heat. Add the onion and sauté until translucent, about 5 minutes. Then add the bell pepper, pineapple, edamame, and baby corn and cook until the mixture is heated through, about 10 minutes.

Add the sauce, green peas, and cold rice and cook, stirring constantly so nothing sticks. Once the rice is hot, the peas should be cooked, and it's ready to serve. That should take 5 to 10 minutes.

Fancy Bean Substitutes: Scarlet Runner, Tepary, Good Mother Stallard

YIELD: 6 servings

PER 2-CUP (455 G) SERVING WITH EDAMAME: 391.0 calories; 9.8 g total fat; 1.2 g saturated fat; 13.9 g protein; 63.7 g carbohydrate; 10.4 g dietary fiber; 0 mg cholesterol.

TOTAL PREP TIME: 20 minutes

TOTAL COOKING TIME: 20 to 25 minutes

Oven Chickpea and Seasonal Veggie Biryani

▶ SOY-FREE ▶ GLUTEN-FREE ▶ OIL-FREE OPTION*

I love dishes I can make the night before, keep in the fridge, and then pop in the oven when I get home from work. This is one of those. You could even make a second one and keep it in the freezer for dinner another night!

1 to 2 tablespoons (15 to 28 ml) olive oil (*use water or broth)

½ small onion, minced

2 cloves garlic, minced

1 teaspoon garam masala

1 teaspoon ground cumin

1 teaspoon coriander

½ teaspoon turmeric

½ teaspoon ground cinnamon

1 tablespoon (8 g) grated ginger

1½ cups (270 g) diced tomatoes or 1 can (14.5 ounces, or 410 g)

½ cup (120 ml) water

4 cups (weight will vary) mixed seasonal veggies, diced or cut into small pieces

1½ cups (246 g) cooked chickpeas or 1 can (15 ounces, or 425 g), rinsed and drained

½ cup (75 g) raisins

6 cups (1.2 kg) cooked long-grain brown rice

....

YIELD: 8 servings

PER 1½-CUP (340 G) SERVING: 332.0 calories; 4.0 g total fat; 0.2 g saturated fat; 9.0 g protein; 73.0 g carbohydrate; 7.3 g dietary fiber; 0 mg cholesterol.

TOTAL PREP TIME: 20 minutes

TOTAL COOKING TIME: 35 to 45 minutes

Preheat the oven to 350°F (180°C, or gas mark 4). Oil an 11 x 8-inch (28 x 20 cm) baking dish *or use a nonstick pan.

Heat the oil in a large saucepan over medium heat. Add the onion and cook until translucent, about 5 minutes. Add the garlic, garam masala, cumin, coriander, turmeric, and cinnamon and sauté a minute or two more until the spices become more fragrant.

Add the ginger, tomatoes, water, and any long-cooking veggies. Cover and cook until the veggies can just be pierced with a fork, but are not completely cooked. They will cook more in the oven. Then add any delicate or quick-cooking veggies, the chickpeas, and the raisins and cook, uncovered, for 3 to 5 minutes.

Spread half of the rice in the bottom of the baking dish, spread the vegetable mixture on top, and then spread the remaining rice on top. Bake for 20 to 30 minutes until the rice is warm. (This will take a longer if the rice was cold from the fridge.)

Serving Suggestions & Variations

Seasonal Veggie Ideas:

• **SPRING:** Asparagus, fava beans, baby turnips, greens, carrots

• **SUMMER:** Eggplant, bell pepper, summer squash, corn

• **FALL:** Sweet potato, greens, winter squash, beets and beet greens

• **WINTER:** Turnips, rutabagas, bok choy, cabbage, collards, potato

Cornbread-Topped Casserole

▶ SOY-FREE OPTION* ▶ GLUTEN-FREE OPTION** ▶ OIL-FREE OPTION***

This is one of the first dishes I made when I went meatless almost thirty years ago.

FOR THE CASSEROLE FILLING

4½ cups (1 kg) cooked beans—a combo of kidney, black, and pinto—or 3 cans (15 ounces, or 425 g each), rinsed and drained

1½ cups (270 g) cooked diced tomatoes or 1 can (14.5 ounces, or 410 g)

½ to 1 teaspoon jalapeño salt or powder or 1 fresh jalapeño, seeded and minced

½ teaspoon ground cumin

½ teaspoon oregano

½ teaspoon chili powder

½ teaspoon granulated garlic or 2 cloves garlic, minced

¼ teaspoon chipotle powder or liquid smoke

¼ teaspoon guajillo powder or your favorite chile powder

FOR THE CORNBREAD TOPPING

1½ cups (355 ml) unsweetened non-dairy milk (*use soy-free)

2 tablespoons (14 g) ground flaxseeds mixed with ¼ cup (60 ml) warm water

1 cup (140 g) cornmeal

½ cup (60 g) whole wheat pastry flour (**use gluten-free)

½ teaspoon baking powder

¼ teaspoon baking soda

¼ teaspoon salt

Preheat the oven to 350°F (180°C, or gas mark 4). Oil an 11 x 8-inch (28 x 20 cm) casserole pan ***or use a nonstick pan.

To make the filling, mix all the ingredients together in a large bowl and then spread the mix in the prepared pan.

To make the cornbread topping, combine the milk and water in one bowl and the cornmeal, flour, baking powder, baking soda, and salt in another bowl. Then add the wet ingredients to the dry, mix well, and spread evenly over the filling in the pan.

Bake, uncovered, for 45 to 60 minutes or until the middle of the cornbread is firm.

Serving Suggestions & Variations

Add more veggies or switch up the beans depending on what you have.

Fancy Bean Substitutes: Rio Zape, Goat's Eye, Cranberry, Black Calypso, Vaquero

....

YIELD: 6 servings

PER SERVING: 306.2 calories; 3.2 g total fat; 0.3 g saturated fat; 14.3 g protein; 57.0 g carbohydrate; 16.5 g dietary fiber; 0 mg cholesterol.

TOTAL PREP TIME: 20 minutes

TOTAL COOKING TIME: 45 to 60 minutes

9

BEAN-A-LICIOUS SWEET TREATS

Desserts That Love Beans

Beans work great in desserts. If you use puréed white beans or red lentils, they fade into the background flavor-wise, but they come to the forefront with moistness and nutritional goodness. It's what makes many of these desserts low in fat, with no added oil. If you weren't hooked on beans before, these sweets will change your mind.

Although beans make baked goods moist and yummy, they won't be quite as light and fluffy as traditional baked goods.

Feel free to substitute your favorite sweetener for the cane sugar or agave nectar. Just add liquid or flour as needed to make up the difference.

Double-Chocolate Devil's Food Cookies

▶ SOY-FREE OPTION* ▶ GLUTEN-FREE OPTION** ▶ OIL-FREE OPTION***

These cookies remind me of a chocolate-coated cookie that I ate growing up. They're like little cakes with a surprise burst of chocolate from the chocolate chips throughout. A few testers even snuck some icing between two of them to create whoopie pies!

1½ cups (180 g) whole wheat pastry flour (**use gluten-free)

½ cup (40 g) unsweetened cocoa powder

1 teaspoon baking soda

¼ teaspoon salt

1½ cups (258 g) cooked black beans or 1 can (15 ounces, or 425 g), rinsed and drained

1 tablespoon (7 g) ground flaxseed mixed with 3 tablespoons (45 ml) warm water

1 cup (235 ml) unsweetened nondairy milk (*use soy-free)

½ cup (115 g) brown sugar

½ cup (100 g) granulated sugar

1 teaspoon vanilla extract

1½ cups (263 g) vegan chocolate chips

::

YIELD: 36 small cookies

PER COOKIE: 109.0 calories; 3.2 g total fat; 1.2 g saturated fat; 2.1 g protein; 19.8 g carbohydrate; 1.7 g dietary fiber; 0 mg cholesterol.

TOTAL PREP TIME: 15 minutes

TOTAL COOKING TIME: 10 to 12 minutes

Preheat the oven to 350°F (180°C, or gas mark 4). Oil a cookie sheet ***or line with parchment paper. (***If you eat oil-free, please note that your chocolate chips probably do have added oil so you may want to leave them out.)

In a large bowl, combine the flour, cocoa, baking soda, and salt.

In a food processor, add the black beans, flaxseed and water mixture, nondairy milk, both sugars, and vanilla. Blend until smooth.

Add the wet mixture to the dry in the bowl along with the chocolate chips and mix with a wooden spoon until combined. Scoop the cookies using a small cookie scoop (about 1½ tablespoons [22.5 g]) onto the prepared cookie sheet and bake for 10 to 12 minutes or until the cookies look dry on top and spring back when lightly touched.

Serving Suggestions & Variations

Use orange or mint extract in place of the vanilla to give your cookies a delicious twist in flavor.

Pecan Chocolate Chip Chickpea Cookies

▶ SOY-FREE OPTION* ▶ GLUTEN-FREE OPTION** ▶ OIL-FREE OPTION***

I had to try some chickpea cookies with all the Internet buzz about chickpeas and chocolate chips—it seemed that every vegan blog had its own cool version. These cookies are almost cakelike. Monika, one of my gluten-free recipe testers, recommends not using a gluten-free baking mix with chickpea flour because it makes the chickpea flavor overwhelming.

FOR THE DRY INGREDIENTS

1½ cups (180 g) whole wheat pastry flour (**use gluten-free)

1 teaspoon baking powder

1 teaspoon baking soda

¼ teaspoon salt

FOR THE WET INGREDIENTS

1½ cups (246 g) cooked chickpeas or 1 can (15 ounces, or 425 g), rinsed and drained

½ cup (120 ml) nondairy milk (vanilla-flavored works great) (*use soy-free)

2 teaspoons vanilla extract

1 cup (225 g) packed brown sugar

FOR THE MIX-INS

1 cup (110 g) chopped pecans or your favorite nut

1 cup (175 g) vegan chocolate chips (***omit if oil-free or sub out)

Preheat the oven to 350°F (180°C, or gas mark 4). Oil a sheet pan ***or line with parchment paper.

To prepare the dry ingredients, combine the ingredients in a large bowl.

To prepare the wet ingredients, add the ingredients to a food processor and blend until smooth.

Add the wet mixture to the dry in the bowl along with the pecans and chocolate chips. Mix with a wooden spoon until combined.

Scoop the cookies using a small cookie scoop (about 1½ tablespoons [22.5 g]) onto the prepared cookie sheet and bake for 12 to 17 minutes or until the cookies look dry on top and spring back when lightly touched.

::

YIELD: 36 cookies

PER COOKIE: 81.1 calories; 3.4 g total fat; 1.0 g saturated fat; 1.4 g protein; 12.6 g carbohydrate; 1.5 g dietary fiber; 0 mg cholesterol.

TOTAL PREP TIME: 20 minutes

TOTAL COOKING TIME: 12 to 17 minutes

Black-Eyed Pea-nut Butter Pie

▶ SOY-FREE OPTION* ▶ GLUTEN-FREE OPTION**

I love having a black-eyed pea dessert for my New Year's Day party. I get a kick out of surprising everyone with the secret ingredient after they've eaten a slice.

1½ cups (248 g) cooked black-eyed peas or 1 can (15 ounces, or 425 g), rinsed and drained

½ cup (130 g) peanut butter

¼ cup (80 g) agave nectar

2 tablespoons (28 ml) nondairy milk (*use soy-free)

¼ cup (44 g) vegan chocolate chips, minced

9-inch (23 cm) store-bought no-bake chocolate cookie crust (**use gluten-free)

In a food processor, purée the black-eyed peas, peanut butter, agave nectar, and nondairy milk until smooth.

Pour the bean mixture into a bowl and mix in half of the minced chocolate chips. Scrape the filling into the no-bake pie crust and sprinkle the top with the rest of the minced chocolate chips. Chill in the fridge for 1 to 2 hours and then serve.

YIELD: 8 servings

PER SERVING: 191.3 calories; 10.5 g total fat; 2.9 g saturated fat; 5.5 g protein; 22.5 g carbohydrate; 3.5 g dietary fiber; 0 mg cholesterol.

TOTAL PREP TIME: 15 minutes

Serving Suggestions & Variations

Make an oil-free version by ditching the crust and serving it parfait-style in nice glasses.

Ginger Red Bean Popsicles

▶ SOY-FREE OPTION* ▶ GLUTEN-FREE
▶ OIL-FREE

Red bean ice cream was my first introduction to using beans in a dessert recipe. This is that idea veganized and in frozen pop form. The sweetness of red beans combined with the ginger-infused coconut milk is perfect for a hot summer day.

1 can (14 ounces, or 400 ml) light coconut milk

1 cup (170 g) Sweet Red Bean Paste (page 27)

½ cup (120 ml) nondairy milk (plain or vanilla) (*use soy-free)

1 tablespoon (8 g) grated fresh ginger

Purée the ingredients together in a food processor or blender. Pour into frozen pop molds and freeze overnight.

....

YIELD: 6 large pops

PER POP: 131.5 calories; 1.8 g total fat; 0.9 g saturated fat; 9.8 g protein; 18.4 g carbohydrate; 1.3 g dietary fiber; 0 mg cholesterol.

TOTAL PREP TIME: 10 minutes

Black Bean Fudgesicles ▶

▶ SOY-FREE ▶ GLUTEN-FREE ▶ OIL-FREE

These healthier fudgesicles still taste like your childhood favorites.

1½ cups (258 g) cooked black beans or 1 can (15 ounces, or 425 g), rinsed and drained

1 can (14 ounces, or 400 ml) light coconut milk

¼ cup (20 g) unsweetened cocoa powder

3 tablespoons (60 g) agave nectar

2 teaspoons vanilla extract

Purée all the ingredients in a food processor until smooth. There will be some black flecks from the black bean skins. I think they look like chocolate flecks, but you can strain the mixture through a cheesecloth if you like.

Fill your frozen pop molds about seven-eighths full of the mixture. Freeze for several hours or overnight before serving.

....

YIELD: 6 large pops

PER POP: 150.4 calories; 4.5 g total fat; 3.4 g saturated fat; 4.6 g protein; 20.0 g carbohydrate; 2.0 g dietary fiber; 0 mg cholesterol.

TOTAL PREP TIME: 10 minutes

Serving Suggestions & Variations:

• Make these for grown-ups only and add a tablespoon or two (15 to 28 ml) of your favorite liquor. Grand Marnier goes great with chocolate!

• No pop molds? You can use small paper cups with wooden sticks or even an ice-cube tray with toothpicks. Don't add the sticks until the mixture is about halfway frozen or they will just fall to the side and not be very useful.

Vanilla and Rose Water Parfaits

▶ SOY-FREE OPTION* ▶ OIL-FREE ▶ GLUTEN-FREE OPTION**

The pudding in these parfaits is thick and tastes almost like cheesecake. Sandwiched in between layers of vanilla cookie crumbs, it's something all your dinner guests will want seconds of. It's a great mini dessert to serve in shot glasses at your next party.

1 cup (230 g) vanilla vegan yogurt (*use coconut yogurt)

1 cup (192 g) cooked red lentils

1 container (12.3 ounces, or 349 g) silken tofu

1 tablespoon (15 ml) rose water

1 teaspoon vanilla extract

2 tablespoons (40 g) agave nectar (more if using plain yogurt)

3 cups (360 g) vanilla cookie crumbs (**use gluten-free)

::

YIELD: 8 parfaits

PER PARFAIT: 124.1 calories; 3.1 g total fat; 0 g saturated fat; 6.0 g protein; 17.8 g carbohydrate; 2.3 g dietary fiber; 0 mg cholesterol.

TOTAL PREP TIME: 20 minutes

Add everything except for the cookie crumbs to a food processor and purée for about 8 minutes. Stop every few minutes and scrape down the side of the bowl to make sure it all gets incorporated.

In eight 10-ounce (280 g) custard cups or in shot glasses to make minis, layer the crumbs on the bottom, add a layer of the tofu mixture, then more crumbs, another layer of tofu, and end by completely covering the top with the rest of the cookie crumbs.

The mixture will thicken up when you refrigerate the parfaits, so put them in the fridge at least 2 hours before serving. They will keep, covered, for a few days.

Serving Suggestions & Variations

Use different extract flavors, add unsweetened cocoa powder, or stir in various liquors to make an unlimited amount of flavors. Graham crackers and chocolate cookies make great crumb layers as well.

Chocolate Cardamom Cake (Mini Bundts)

▶ SOY-FREE OPTION* ▶ GLUTEN-FREE OPTION**

What's not to love about pre-portioned moist chocolate cake? I make a batch, keep two mini cakes to eat, and freeze six for later. And if you are being really good, you can share one with someone special after dinner.

FOR THE DRY INGREDIENTS

1½ cups (180 g) whole wheat pastry flour (**use gluten-free)

¾ cup (150 g) sugar

½ cup (40 g) unsweetened cocoa powder

1 teaspoon baking powder

1 teaspoon cardamom

½ teaspoon baking soda

¼ teaspoon salt

FOR THE WET INGREDIENTS

1½ cups (269 g) cooked white beans or 1 can (15 ounces, or 425 g), rinsed and drained

1½ cups (355 ml) nondairy milk (vanilla-flavored works great) (*use soy-free)

1 tablespoon (7 g) ground flaxseed mixed with 2 tablespoons (28 ml) warm water

1 teaspoon vanilla extract

½ teaspoon almond extract

Preheat the oven to 350°F (180°C, or gas mark 4). Oil 8 mini bundt pans, custard cups, or other baking pans. (Adjust the cooking time if you use something larger or smaller.)

To prepare the dry ingredients, mix all the ingredients in a large bowl.

To prepare the wet ingredients, add all the ingredients to a food processor and blend until smooth. Add the wet mixture to the dry in the bowl and mix with a wooden spoon until combined.

Fill the bundt pans about two-thirds full with the batter and bake for 20 to 25 minutes or until the cakes spring back when lightly touched.

Serving Suggestions & Variations

Vary the extract flavor and add in some nuts or chocolate chips to create your own one-of-a-kind cake.

....

YIELD: 8 mini bundts or 10-ounce (280 g) mini baking dishes

PER MINI BUNDT: 228.8 calories; 2.4 g total fat; 0.5 g saturated fat; 6.7 g protein; 49.3 g carbohydrate; 9.8 g dietary fiber; 0 mg cholesterol.

TOTAL PREP TIME: 15 minutes

TOTAL COOKING TIME: 20 to 25 minutes

Coconut Pecan Blondies

▶ SOY-FREE OPTION* ▶ GLUTEN-FREE OPTION**

These blondies are for special treats. These are not oil-free or sugar-free, but they taste like butterscotch with flecks of coconut and pecans, so they are well worth the splurge!

FOR THE DRY INGREDIENTS

1 cup (120 g) whole wheat pastry flour (**use gluten-free)

1 tablespoon (14 g) Ener-G egg replacer

½ teaspoon baking soda

½ teaspoon salt

FOR THE WET INGREDIENTS

1 cup (250 g) cooked white beans or red lentils

½ cup (120 ml) nondairy milk (unsweetened vanilla works great) (*use soy-free)

¼ cup (60 ml) olive oil or canola oil

¼ cup (60 g) brown sugar

¼ cup (50 g) granulated sugar

2 teaspoons vanilla extract

FOR THE MIX-INS

½ cup (43 g) shredded coconut

½ cup (55 g) chopped pecans

Preheat the oven to 350°F (180°C, or gas mark 4). Oil an 8 x 8-inch (20 x 20 cm) square brownie pan.

To prepare the dry ingredients, mix all the ingredients in a large mixing bowl.

To prepare the wet ingredients, add the wet ingredients to a food processor and process until smooth. This will take about 3 to 5 minutes.

Add the wet mixture to the dry in the bowl and mix well. Then mix in the coconut and pecans.

Scrape into the prepared pan and bake for 25 to 35 minutes or until the blondies look dry on top and spring back when lightly touched. You want the middle to be a little soft because it will bake more as it cools. Let cool and then cut into 12 pieces.

....

YIELD: 12 servings

PER BLONDIE: 238.3 calories; 15.0 g total fat; 7.0 g saturated fat; 3.3 g protein; 25.0 g carbohydrate; 3.9 g dietary fiber; 0 mg cholesterol.

TOTAL PREP TIME: 15 minutes

TOTAL COOKING TIME: 25 to 35 minutes

Cherry Basil Crumble Bars

▶ SOY-FREE ▶ GLUTEN-FREE OPTION* ▶ OIL-FREE OPTION**

It's beans that allow the crust to be oil-free, but it's the cherries and basil that make them extra special.

FOR THE CRUST

1 cup (179 g) cooked white beans

½ cup (55 g) slivered almonds

½ cup (48 g) rolled oats (*use gluten-free)

½ cup (60 g) whole wheat pastry flour (*use gluten-free)

¼ cup (80 g) agave nectar

FOR THE TOPPING

½ cup (90 g) cooked white beans

½ cup (55 g) slivered almonds

½ cup (48 g) rolled oats (*use gluten-free)

½ cup (60 g) whole wheat pastry flour (*use gluten-free)

¼ cup (80 g) agave nectar

FOR THE FILLING

2 cups (310 g) pitted or frozen cherries

¼ cup (6 g) fresh basil

¼ to ½ cup (80 to 160 g) agave nectar, depending on tartness of fruit

½ teaspoon arrowroot powder or cornstarch

:::

YIELD: 12 bars

PER BAR: 268.2 calories; 7.4 g total fat; 0.6 g saturated fat; 7.0 g protein; 43.1 g carbohydrate; 6.7 g dietary fiber; 0 mg cholesterol.

TOTAL PREP TIME: 30 minutes (less if not using cherries)

TOTAL COOKING TIME: 20 to 30 minutes

Preheat the oven to 350°F (180°C, or gas mark 4). Oil an 11 x 8-inch (28 x 20 cm) casserole pan **or use a nonstick pan.

To make the crust, add all the ingredients to a food processor and blend until the consistency of large cornmeal. Press into the bottom of the pan.

To make the topping, add all the ingredients to the food processor bowl before you wash it and pulse until the almonds are broken up well. Pour into a bowl and set aside.

To make the filling, you can still use the unwashed food processor and add all the ingredients. Double-check that all the cherry pits have been removed. You'll hear them in the food processor if any slipped by. Spread the puréed filling over the crust and then crumble the topping over that.

Bake, uncovered, for 20 to 30 minutes or until the topping browns and the filling has set up. Let cool and then cut into 12 bars.

Serving Suggestions & Variations

Try with different seasonal fruits and herbs or spices: apple cinnamon, blueberry mint, or even strawberry basil.

Chocolate Summer Squash Cake

▶ SOY-FREE OPTION* ▶ GLUTEN-FREE OPTION** ▶ OIL-FREE OPTION***

If you've ever grown summer squash, you know that you run out of ways to use it before it even slows down. This recipe is a way to use up all the extra, and you can freeze some of this cake to eat in the winter when you're dreaming about summer squash.

FOR THE DRY INGREDIENTS

1½ cups (180 g) whole wheat pastry flour (**use gluten-free)

½ cup (40 g) unsweetened cocoa powder

1 teaspoon baking soda

½ teaspoon salt

FOR THE WET INGREDIENTS

1½ cups (269 g) cooked white beans or 1 can (15 ounces, or 425 g), rinsed and drained

½ cup (120 ml) nondairy milk (*use soy-free)

½ cup (160 g) agave nectar

2 tablespoons ground flaxseed mixed with ¼ cup (60 ml) warm water

2 teaspoons vanilla extract

FOR THE MIX-INS

2 cups (240 g) grated summer squash

1 cup (175 g) vegan chocolate chips (***omit if oil-free of sub out)

Preheat the oven to 350°F (180°C, or gas mark 4). Oil a 9-inch (23 cm) loaf pan or a 9 x 13-inch (23 x 33 cm) pan, depending on whether you want a loaf or cake squares, ***or use a nonstick pan. (***If you eat oil-free, please note that your chocolate chips probably do have added oil.)

To prepare the dry ingredients, combine all the ingredients in a large mixing bowl and make a well in the middle.

To prepare the wet ingredients, add all the ingredients to a food processor and purée until smooth. Then scrape into the large mixing bowl with the dry ingredients and gently mix until combined.

Mix in the summer squash and chocolate chips. Pour into the prepared baking pan. Bake for about 25 minutes (for a rectangular pan) to 50 minutes (for a loaf pan) or until a knife inserted into the center comes out clean.

:::

YIELD: 12 slices

PER SLICE: 257.0 calories; 7.7 g total fat; 3.9 g saturated fat; 7.0 g protein; 46.0 g carbohydrate; 7.1 g dietary fiber; 0 mg cholesterol.

TOTAL PREP TIME: 15 minutes

TOTAL COOKING TIME: 25 to 50 minutes

Resource Guide

If you have access to a Whole Foods store or a co-op you are likely to find more heirloom beans there than ever before. I've also found them at larger specialty food stores. But if you live far from a city, you can find all the heirloom beans you could ever want online. Here are a few sources that I've found.

Rancho Gordo

(www.ranchogordo.com) My favorite online bean source. While you're there, be sure to pick up some of the chili powder—I used a whole jar writing this book! Rancho Gordo also works with farmers in Mexico to preserve native heirlooms there, so the company has good food and a good heart.

Purcell Mountain Farms

(www.purcellmountainfarms.com) A good selection of organic beans and located in Idaho. Their online store is very easy to order from.

Zürsun Idaho Heirloom Beans

(www.zursunbeans.com) Sells mostly on the West Coast, but check the list just in case you can get some in your area. It's worth a trip to the site just to look at the detailed photos of many heirloom beans.

Cayuga Pure Organics

(www.cporganics.com) Located in upstate New York, they use sustainable farming practices, and sell beans in Ithaca and at New York City greenmarkets.

Native Seeds

(www.nativeseeds.org) A nonprofit organization dedicated to conserving and nurturing the traditional agricultural heritage of the Greater Southwest. You can get beans to eat and to use as seeds to grow your own heirlooms.

Seed Savers Exchange

(www.seedsavers.org) A great source for all heirloom seeds with a huge collection. In addition to almost any seeds you'd want to plant, they have yummy heirloom beans for you to cook up for dinner.

Spice Resources

I love to try different herbs and spices. I have a huge spice drawer in my kitchen, but that doesn't stop them from having their own shelf in the pantry and a place in the cupboard for the overflow. I admit it—I'm a spice geek. I can't resist trying a new flavored salt, and if I spot an herb or a spice I've never seen before, it must come home with me.

I've tried to keep most of the recipes pretty basic, but there may be a few spices in these recipes that you aren't as familiar with yet. If you have a co-op or place that sells bulk spices in your area, then that should be your first stop. You can get amounts smaller than a teaspoon so you aren't investing a fortune in something you might not even like.

Indian groceries are a perfect and inexpensive source for spices. The kala namak salt there is less than one-fourth of the price I paid at a fancy olive oil store. Yes, I paid $12 for my first kala namak salt, but I've replaced it for much less and it's the same thing.

Hispanic groceries are a playground of fresh and dried chiles. You can toast the whole dried chiles in the oven until crumbly, but not burnt, and grind them in a spice grinder for the freshest chile powder you will ever taste!

My Spice Sage

(www.myspicesage.com) This is the online spice shop that I use the most. They have tons of exotic blends and a great source for Indian spices and blends.

They also have free shipping in the United States with a minimum purchase. For a slightly larger purchase, you also get whatever the featured premium spice is for free. I've received saffron and smoked salt in the past; it changes regularly. Also, you get to pick a free 1-ounce (28 g) spice from a huge list with every order. I've received spice blends for particular Indian dishes and free samples of things I wanted to try. You can see why it's become my favorite and why my spices are overflowing everywhere!

Savory Spice Shop

(www.savoryspiceshop.com) A small chain, with an online store if there's not one in your area. Their extracts are amazing!

Penzeys Spices

(www.penzeys.com) Another chain that's chock full of choices.

Frontier Natural Products Co-Op

(www.frontiercoop.com) The brand you'll usually find in bulk bins locally, but you can also order online.

ACKNOWLEDGMENTS

Amanda Waddell was a huge support and helped me shape this book into what it is. Many thanks to Kevin Mulroy for believing in me and this book, editor Renae Haines, proofreader Marilyn Kecyk, and the rest of the Fair Winds team for all their hard work.

I want to thank Nava Atlas for unsuspectedly leading me to my agent. I am honored that Lisa and Sally Ekus chose to represent me and am grateful for how wonderful they have been to work with.

The beautiful photography is the work of photographer Renée Comet. It was my pleasure to finally get to work with her.

My fearless testers have my sincere gratitude: Rochelle Arvizo, Monika Soria Caruso, Kimber Cherry, Julie Cross, Jamie Coble, Cheryl Foley, Faith Hood, Mary Harris, Ruth Zagg, and Stephanie Stanesby. A salute to all Cheryl's coworkers at Novelist who fearlessly tasted the food I sent them and to all my friends who knew there were beans in everything they ate at my house.

Thanks to Cara Connors and Karen Levy for doing a great editing job. I am so thrilled with Debbie Berne's amazing design for this book.

Rochelle Arvizo, Julie Cross, and Ellen Foreman went beyond their tester and taster roles. I owe you all many pounds of heirloom beans for all your efforts!

I can't possibly thank Cheryl Purser enough for not only taking care of me and the animals but also for actually moving our whole household while I wrote this book. She's still a picky eater, but she was excited to find out I was writing a bean book. Finally something she loves!

ABOUT THE AUTHOR

Kathy Hester, author of the bestselling cookbook *The Vegan Slow Cooker*, loves to show people how easy it is to cook.

She is the founder of www.healthyslowcooking.com and the vegan blogger for Key Ingredient (www.keyingredient.com/blog/bloggers/kathy-hester). She also writes for *Chickpea Vegan Quarterly* and teaches vegan cooking classes.

She has more slow cookers than one person should own, plus enough beans in the pantry to last at least a year, too. She resides in Durham, North Carolina, with a grown-up picky eater in a quirky 1970s modernist house. Her new house is big enough for the cats and the dog to finally all get along, and now they all hang out on the deck together while she writes.

Index